...ened on the Way to Energy Independence

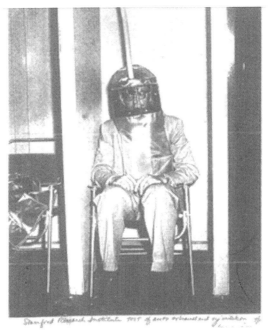

In the old days, Stanford Research Institute worked on the big air pollution problem of the day— irritated, red eyes from diesel exhaust. This volunteer is having diesel exhaust pumped into the hood to see if it irritates his eyes... And these were the good old days.

Please visit us at
www.EnergyLaughs.com

A Funny Thing Happened on the Way to Energy Independence

The first energy or environmental book that makes no point and doesn't ask you to think.

by Robert Danziger

Front cover by Mike Kazaleh
Illustrations by Mike Kazaleh, Juan Ibanez, and Arno Baernhoft

iv

Published by Robert Danziger through
CreateSpace

For further information please contact:
EnergyLaughs@me.com

Or go to the website:
www.EnergyLaughs.com

First published in 2010 by Robert Danziger

ISBN 1450557295

LCCN 2010901478

Contents

Part 5
Music Man

X

Conclusion

Preface

A Funny Thing Happened on the Way to Energy Independence seeks readers on all sides of the energy/environmental debate who like to laugh. Energy is serious, but Mom taught me to look for the funny.

I'm one of the ghosts of alternative energy past. We ghosts were riding the Wild West putting in windmills and solar systems, cogeneration and biofuel plants, and picking a lot of the low-hanging energy-saving fruits and nuts. A pretty good case can be made that we are responsible for saving around 12 billion barrels of oil and 26 billion tons of greenhouse gases. I think it's the biggest energy savings in history, but there's no shortage of opinions about energy and environment.

Here I share alternative energy's locker-room stories. *A Funny Thing Happened on the Way to Energy Independence* might be the first energy and environmental book that makes no point and doesn't ask you to think – but you can if you want to.

Condensed History of Energy

ANCIENT EGYPT: Wind, water and animal power.

Animals like Oxen pulled the carts and the plows. The power of the Nile was captured to lift water and turn the mills. Wind in the sails moved King Tut's boats.

I thought about Egypt and its hieroglyphs when it was time to make the cover for my third CD, "Danz/Beat Live at Leed's." Having recently invented an air pollution control technology called SCONOx, and watched it work at a full-scale power plant, the environment was very much on my mind. I was trying to make the power plant act like a tree to the environment – take in water, air and nutrients, and produce stuff like wood and oxygen. We had just made a major step in the right direction.

One of the songs on the album is called "Demand Clean Air." One of the vocalists was Ellie Sherman, an artist and specialist in ancient and lost languages. On the recording she says, "Demand Clean Air" in almost 20 different languages. Turns out the Egyptians had dozens of words for air so one word meant "wind from the north," and another might mean "wind that pushes the boats."

We picked, "The Wind of the Cow."

RENAISSANCE ITALY - LEONARDO DA VINCI: Invented solar energy concentrators.

The very first solar energy equipment manufacturing I saw was a factory east of Los Angeles that made solar energy concentrators and bullets. The first concentrators used in the United States, they made steam for a laundry just a couple of blocks from the Rose Parade.

1898, F.A. PORSCHE: Builds and races the first hybrid cars.

As this young century reaches its teenage years, electric and hybrid cars are expected to be "the next big thing." Every major manufacturer is readying models that will rely more on electricity than in the past. When I worked at Jet Propulsion Lab in the late 70's we were a Lead Center for electric car development. The old joke back then was that if you wanted to find an electric car, just find the trailer it came in and it won't be far away. Now the Tesla goes hundreds of miles on a charge and can be recharged very quickly. The Chevy Volt with its range extender (another grandbaby of the Porsche design) has the potential to go over 500 miles with a few tweaks.

FOSSIL FUELS: Oil and coal fuelled the industrial revolution, and virtually every industrial power derives the bulk of its wealth from readily accessible and relatively cheap oil, gas and coal. In Saudi Arabia, where oil would bubble out of the ground and roll downhill to waiting oil tankers, its oil minister warned OPEC to keep prices low because "The stone age didn't end because they ran out of stones." In a strange twist, Exxon and Saudi Arabia both now project world oil demand will decline, as more money was spent on alternative electricity sources than conventional energy for the first time (2008). Who knows? Maybe the fossil fuel era won't end because they ran out of fossil fuels. I used to predict oil and gas prices for a living. Glad I don't have to do that anymore.

- - - - - - - - - -

I welcome your comments, questions, jokes and stories at www.EnergyLaughs.com. And remember – the next time someone preaches at you about some energy or environmental thing – forget whatever they said, and tell them a funny story. If you don't have one, feel free to use one of mine.

Pepper Car (Juan Ibanez)

Part 1

The Beginning

8

Chapter 1

We Get It

This is a story about the funny things in my career, which just happens to be the alternative energy and environment business. "Funny?" you are thinking? Energy and environment? Funny?!

Fair point. Did you hear the one about acid mine drainage, climate change, and smog going into a bar? Haven't heard it?

Just kidding. It's not funny yet. Doomsday lite, please.

I was a player in the alternative energy and environmental technology world for the last thirty years or so, often on the bleeding edge of the front lines. Been there, done that, studied it, built it. I'm not as smart as I sometimes think I am, but I'm plenty smart to understand this area. And I did bring an extra dash of creativity not usually found in the energy business. If you think energy and environment are grim subjects, trust me, alternative energy can be a cruel mistress, and someone's been a very, very bad boy. But, as Mom told us:

"If you don't want any aches or pains or trouble in life, die young."

So enough with the doom and the gloom and the race to predict ever-greater catastrophe. WE GET IT. There's a problem. Chicken Little got her friends eaten for three false alarms. We've heard a lot more than three false alarms from all sides—many of us have heard thousands. While there are truly outstanding people on both sides, these days we often hear from ill-informed wing nuts intent on shouting everybody else down. Are you as tired of the anger and rhetoric and posturing and exaggeration as I am? Has it started taking on the character of a crazy man wearing a sandwich board and preaching that the end is nigh? Does it feel like you're wading through a pool full of porcupines and cactus?

Hopefully, this book will be an antidote for you.

OK, there's a problem. Now let's fix it. That's my business—fixing it.

Starting with an initial dream of making the energy world clean and cheap, I suffered the ups and downs of business and life, had some big successes, learned some lessons the hard way. All in all, I wouldn't trade it for anything.

- - - - - - - - - -

The stories told here are mostly true. Names were changed to protect the humiliated, and sometimes whole facts were "modified" to make for a better story. Or a funnier story. Or at least less personally incriminating.

But there is a kernel of truth in all these stories. Sometimes a whole cob.

- - - - - - - - - -

Mom is the one who taught me to look for the funny in things, and she is the best joke teller I know. Mom loves a good, or not so good, joke and will tell it to absolutely anybody and everybody. In times of crisis, the one thing you can be sure of is that the hospital room with laughter spilling out of it is ours. For example, my sister, Ronna, had a baby, and a few months later she was sitting with Mom and going on and on about the joys of breast-feeding. Mom looked over at me and said, "Don't get any ideas."

When I was growing up, my mother had an abstract relationship with school lunches. Not exactly strong in the culinary arts, food hygiene, or sympathy to my wailing, Mom thought of cooking the way most people think of mulching, changing the leach field for the septic tank, gynecological exams, dental visits, and spring cleaning. Boy, did my sister and I look forward to TV dinner night.

One year, before the first day of school Mom asked me what I wanted for lunch. "Tuna sandwich," I replied. She made 180 tuna sandwiches (on Wonder Bread!), put them all in the freezer, and told me to take one each morning when I left for school. Of course, within a week the bread had turned to slime and the tuna to fishy crystals. Though I was the biggest guy in the whole school, even physical intimidation didn't facilitate trades with the other kids for their lunches. Within two weeks I was actually told by another fifth grader that I could beat him up but he wasn't going to give me his sandwich, and he certainly didn't want mine.

Humor was a big factor in my career. I was one of the guys who always had a few jokes to tell. I keep a list of my favorite jokes in my wallet and add new ones that I hear. I brought a lot of negatives to my career, and having a joke ready got me past some tough situations because we could connect around something funny. For example, one day I was complaining to a mentor about people being mean to me, and he drawled, "You're the only fat, Jewish, non-Republican, environmentalist lawyer from California in the energy business, what the f— did you expect?"

Why with the Music Stuff?

You will also be reading quite a bit about music in this book. I never made much money at it, but I've been active in music almost my whole life, recording and performing at the same time as doing my energy work. So don't be surprised by all the music references.

On a Serious Note

I make my living doing serious energy stuff, but this book is about anything but that. If you want to get serious about the study of energy or environment, buy almost any other book. This one is for fun.

Chapter 2

JPL and Caltech Days

After graduating from law school, my professional career began at Jet Propulsion Laboratory (JPL) in Pasadena. Home of the U.S. deep space exploration program, JPL was called upon to work its magic leading the alternative energy programs essential to winning the "moral equivalent of war" due to oil embargos and the deep recessions that followed.

The California Institute of Technology, popularly known as Caltech, is the "academic home" of Jet Propulsion Laboratory and runs it as a national laboratory, mostly for NASA. Caltech is one of the elite universities, like Stanford, MIT, and Harvard. It has a small enrollment of fewer than one thousand students and about the same number of teachers.

Einstein taught there, as did Linus Pauling, Richard Feynman, and Murray Gell-Mann. Nobel Prize winners get special parking places.

JPL has about six thousand employees, primarily space scientists and engineers, and it's the place that managed the exploration of our solar system for the

United States. Starting with the moon, JPL has sent satellites to all the planets, unless you include Pluto, which was demoted to a space rock and is no longer considered a planet.

JPL has taken incredible pictures and made amazing sound recordings of Mars, Jupiter, Saturn, Uranus, Neptune, Venus, Mercury, the sun, and now interstellar space.

Just a few years earlier (1970), the greatest environmental movement in history started when more than 90 percent of ALL the people in the United States ranked clean air and water in their top three political concerns after *Apollo 8* took this picture:

The view of the earth from the moon brought home the fragility of the planet to people in ways that scientific studies and political rhetoric have never equaled. It was a shining moment of bipartisanship I've never seen again but still believe in.

Then, in the mid-1970s, a confluence of several events heightened the world's awareness of energy and environment to levels never seen since. OPEC, after the 1973 Arab-Israeli War, started choking off oil supplies to the United States. Actual gasoline shortages resulted in long lines of cars waiting to buy rationed gas. Oil prices skyrocketed, causing a severe recession combined with sky-high interest rates.

President Carter called the situation the "moral equivalent of war." Seemingly impossible things needed to be achieved for victory in this war—energy independence and a clean environment coupled with prosperity. Solar energy had to be reduced in cost by 99 percent (by 2009, we were 94 percent of the way there) to compete with fossil fuels. A mass-producible electric and hybrid car had to be invented. Natural gas had to be produced from rocks like coal and shale. Giant windmills needed to sprout like cornfields. A thousand other ideas had to be examined, often tried, and then decisions had to be made about their future.

JPL, at that time, had never failed at accomplishing the impossible. Fly to the moon? Fly to Jupiter? Saturn? All done to perfection. Incredibly difficult scientific and engineering systems had to be invented, on a schedule, and had to work under the watchful eye of the people on earth. And JPL had never failed, unlike the other national labs, which had experienced a more normal failure rate.

With this national energy crisis, JPL was called upon to work its magic in interplanetary space exploration on the energy and environment problems of earth. JPL responded by undertaking lead responsibility for solar energy and the electric and hybrid vehicle, and was deeply involved in alternative fuels, underwater nuclear power plants, solar-powered satellites that could beam energy back to earth, and everything in between.

Like many, I dove into this national emergency, and suddenly found myself among JPL's mix of academic and scientific elite who were trying to solve these problems. I had no undergraduate education, let alone a degree, and the highlight from my law school education was a professor giving me a B and commenting:

"That's the highest grade I've ever given to anyone who didn't actually attend my class."

Nevertheless, it was the perfect start for a young kid just out of school to pursue the impossible dream of prosperity coupled with energy independence and a clean environment. JPL expected to achieve the impossible, and that suited me perfectly.

JPL had put together a systems analysis section, to support the scientific and engineering work and to meet the nation's need for policy formulation and analysis. More common today, systems analysis was in its middle childhood at the time.

Systems analysis involves a Noah's ark of professionals, all looking at a challenge from each of their unique perspectives: architects, operations researchers, environmental engineers, economists (lots of economists), lawyers, biologists, anthropologists, geographers—all kinds of people in the same boat.

When systems analysis works right, all these professionals are rowing in the same direction. When it doesn't work right, as my mom observed, **"The smartest people do the dumbest things." That's how I know I'm a genius.**

Chapter 3

My Weird Education and Career Prep

A look of horror spread across the face of my wife's friend, a professor at Stanford, as I described my checkered, out-of-the-box educational history to her. Although, to be fair to myself, I actually am infinitely curious, love to learn, and spent my time away from law classes studying engineering, physics, and a bunch of other things while working two jobs—as a data processing manager and as a musician playing in recording sessions.

The weirdest thing about my education is that, even though I went to law school, passed the bar, developed and taught alternative energy law, worked for and lectured at Jet Propulsion Laboratory and Stanford, I went to undergraduate school for only three months and then became a professional musician. After barely making a living as a musician, I took and passed the college equivalency exam and got into law school.

I first tried Mid-Valley College of Law—the "best law school on Van Nuys Boulevard"—a school distinguished by the fact that not one of its students ever passed the bar exam. I eventually transferred to a real law school, Whittier Law School, which wasn't as funny.

And, as the professor who gave me the B noted, I didn't exactly go when I went, if you know what I mean. I would stay just long enough to be counted for attendance purposes and then get out of there as fast as possible.

What did get my complete focus was an alternative energy device I had invented just a few months before starting law school. It used solar, wind, and biomass energy to supply all the electricity a home needed, with some left over. I was very curious, since I was in law school anyway, about what laws and regulations my invention might encounter.

My invention featured a windmill and solar system that both produced heat. The heat went into a storage tank that also used a burner for natural gas and biomass (i.e. "bathroom burps") generated around the home. All this stuff was incorporated into a prefabricated garage. Although, as it turned out, not commercially practical because of the size of the heat storage required, it was a great platform for learning about energy because it had more or less every technology and energy product

folded in. Fortunately, the legal and regulatory implications of the device extended into the areas that became the big issues of the next decade.

I was given the freedom at law school to concentrate on and write about alternative energy law, and this was before any such class existed anywhere in the world. As a result, I was one of the first students to study and then teach alternative energy law.

My thanks to Dean Friesen, who declared:

> "When someone is describing the nature of the universe to you, unless they are floating six inches above the ground it's just an opinion."

And later:

> "When two men are discussing the universe, the one thing you can be sure of is that theirs is bigger than yours."[1]

I can't tell you how often those thoughts came in handy…especially when things did not go as expected.

---

[1] The current holders of the "biggest universe" prize have to be the string theory physicists, who have come up with eleven different dimensions, each with their own infinity!

Chapter 4

JPL: Getting the Job

For the first National Renewable Energy Technology Conference, held in Tucson, Arizona, I submitted two papers on solar energy and both were accepted. I had recently graduated from law school and was looking for a job.

When I received the program for the conference, I called the other presenters and tried to subtly sound them out about recommending possible employers. With their recommendations, I interviewed at TRW and Fairchild Semiconductor, both of which were doing early work in solar energy under various federal programs.

One conference speaker was from Jet Propulsion Laboratory. He told me JPL didn't use the normal interview process. Rather, prospective employees were first invited to give a seminar, and if that went well, they were invited back to do a more standard interview. A seminar was organized, and I got paid a couple hundred dollars as well! That was big money for me then.

But first, I needed a topic for my seminar.

As a follow-up to my law review articles and the speeches at the conference, I wondered what would happen if trying to build a gigantic solar energy system. Sort of a giant version of my invention. Such giant solar and wind systems are common around the world now, but none existed back then. What legal problems would they face? How would they finance it? Did different technologies raise different legal issues? Did size matter?

I had recently given a lecture at the University of California, Los Angeles (UCLA) Engineering School based on this study of the legal implications of large solar energy systems making and selling electricity. I decided to title my seminar at JPL "The Legal Implications of a One Megawatt (Five Million Dollar) Solar Power Plant." Unbeknownst to me, JPL had just gotten a contract from Congress to write a report on "The Legal Implications of a One Megawatt Solar Power Plant."

Same name, same subject matter. Sometimes you just seriously luck out. The dream was steaming down the track.

Chapter 5

Give or Take $500 Million

JPL was the lead center in the United States for alternative energy in the late 1970s and early 1980s. One of JPL's responsibilities was to recommend a budget for solar electricity research for the coming year. I was one of the junior staff people on the effort, and we worked day and night for several weeks to prepare three options for the government to consider.

If I remember correctly, the "low" scenario was two billion dollars or so, the "medium" was four and a half billion dollars, and the "aggressive" scenario was seven or eight billion dollars. A Saturday conference call was arranged with the chief of staff for the congressional committee, Henry Eaton, to brief him on our conclusions.

On some of my earlier trips for JPL to Washington, DC, I had gotten to know Henry. We had a few meals together, and he'd helped us out on a bizarre problem we had with the Department of Energy. Congress had allocated ninety-eight million dollars to put solar electric systems on federal buildings. For political reasons too strange to recount here, the Department of

Energy had decided to use the money to put solar-powered fans on outhouses in the middle of national forests.

I'll stop for a moment while you think about that one.

We were in the middle of a national energy crisis and the Department of Energy wanted to put almost one hundred million dollars into outhouse fans?! Henry got the department to change course and install the solar systems in places where they were really needed, which you've probably seen, around remote towers, gates, and harbors.

Anyway, we were all standing around the conference table, senior JPL people briefing congressional staff and leaders, and we junior-staff types getting documents, preparing numbers, and so on. They had been going at it for an hour or so, and the Washington folks focused on the four-and-a-half-billion-dollar program. In the middle of all this, Henry asked,

"Is Bob Danziger there?"

"Yes, I'm here, Henry."

"Bob, is the four-point-five-billion-dollar scenario right? Are the numbers right?"

"Yes, Henry, give or take five hundred million."

"OK, Bob."

And that's what went to Congress.

About an hour later it hit me: give or take five hundred million! I was making $19,500 a year at the time. Give or take five hundred million?

Chapter 6

Perp, Purple, PURPA

A law was passed in 1978 that changed the course of energy history. This law was the focus of that first JPL seminar about the legal implications of big solar energy power plants. Until this law was passed, only public utilities and governments could own power plants in virtually the whole world. Solar energy, wind energy, and energy conservation were not of much interest to them, and many viewed all this alternative energy stuff as a threat. The law was on their side, so they could stop it.

JPL took a keen interest in the new law, which was called the Public Utility Regulatory Policies Act, or PURPA, and I was authorized to write a book about the law and the regulations because of their potential impact on solar technology and other technologies JPL was working on.

The next thirty years proved that the predicted impacts of PURPA largely occurred as expected—enough alternative energy has been installed worldwide to equal one whole United States' worth of electricity production. And almost every one of those companies that opposed alternative energy now supports it.

SWEL and the Beautiful Blonde

When this energy law was passed, making it legal for
companies and individuals to own their own solar,
wind, and other alternative energy power plants, the
regulations and guidelines for implementing it were
put together by the Federal Energy Regulatory
Commission (FERC). FERC is a powerful federal
agency little known to the public, but its influence in
our daily lives is felt every day—unless you don't use
electricity or gas. You could say we get FERC'ed
every day.

As part of the process of implementing the law,
hearings were held in a handful of cities around the
country, and they were dull. Incredibly dull. If you
think your life is dull, try ten days of parsing public
utility law; it'll make you want to be a proofreader for
the white pages of the phone book.

The big hearing, though, the one where the big guns
came out, was in Washington, DC, in the old FERC
offices near DC's Union Train Station, right down the
block from the Capitol. The hearings in Washington
were scheduled for three mind-numbing days and
promised to be a steady drone of lobbyists and

delusions of grandeur. The staff actually had been fun, but the speakers had been snoozers.

And then in walked a gentleman, probably in his late sixties, wearing a white suit, white shoes, white fedora, red silk tie, and gold nugget cuff links. He was rocking an ebony cane with a carved ivory handle and gold inlay. On his arm was a drop-dead gorgeous blonde, probably twenty-eight years old, also dressed in white—white silk dress five inches above the knee, four-inch spike heels, seamed white fishnets, a pin overflowing with white pearls, sparkling diamonds, sapphires, and a large ruby implying a flower. Her wedding ring, in a traditional setting, had a rock the size of a cherry.

They registered to speak and found a spot in the corner to begin the three-day wait. He was one of the last speakers. In the meantime, they'd stroll around the room, he leaning on the cane, and she holding his arm so that her "ampleness" was well framed. We had two choices: we could focus on the speakers—"Section 201 is silent on the propitious opportunity of blah-blah-blah"—or we could look at them, and by them I mean her.

Each day the mystery deepened. Who was he? Who were they? Where were they from? How did that old guy get that girl? They weren't discourteous; we knew they had Southern accents. They nevertheless did not engage in much conversation with the rest of the audience

Finally, after maybe a hundred speakers, he was called upon to make his statement. From the witness chair, he said he was representing SWEL Electricity. That's right, SWEL, the same things our hearts and minds did when we saw that girl.

SWEL, it turned out, was a program started by Oglethorpe Rural Electric Cooperative, the largest in the country, to use the poop from cows, pigs, and other farm animals to make electricity. The idea was that if it took the manure from fifty cows or the pig pies from 120 pigs to power a farm or something, the farmers in the cooperative would each locate that number of animals at a central location, where the manure would be collected and processed into electricity. He wanted to make sure the law didn't prevent that kind of thing.

At the end of his testimony, a commissioner said that he understood the man's concerns, but had a question:

"What does *SWEL* stand for?"

"You take the first two letters of swine, *SW*, and the first two letters of electricity, *EL*, and that's what you get: *SWEL*—Swine Electricity."

- - - - - - - - -

These were the hearings that launched the largest alternative energy, environmental, and economic happening ever in energy, and all it took was a beautiful blonde and a whole bunch of pigs.

Chapter 7

Putting the "Rock" Back in Rocket

Oil isn't always oil. Sometimes it's something like oil that is squeezed out of sand or shale rock or coal. In fact, there's far more of the part of oil that we use (hydrocarbons) in these other things than there is in oil itself.

These gooey or rock-hard types of oil need a lot of water and they pollute, just like oil. Many of us were and are researching ways of bringing up the good stuff, while leaving the bad stuff like greenhouse gases and smog makers deep in the earth. Many of these underground energy conversion systems require very large tunnels to process the rock and collect the oil.

JPL had a program to fund pet projects of scientists and engineers. A JPL engineer came in to present his idea for building gigantic tunnels to our team, which was evaluating grant requests. He noted that big rockets are the same size as train tunnels—the perfect size for large-scale recovery of these oil substitutes. He got the bright idea to build a rocket that went down instead of up.

He excitedly exclaimed:

"What is the earth? It is just *thick space*!"

He was very animated, which is always funny for a guy with pocket protectors and a long-ignored hairdo. But the thick space in this case was between the ears.

He also had the idea of building a tunnel from New York to Los Angeles, two hundred miles beneath the surface (now that's an escalator!), that would have had these trains capable of traveling from coast to coast in half an hour. When I asked him how it worked, he said, "It spends most of the time slowing down."

Chapter 8

Doctors Jump Out of Cakes Too

Congress and the country wanted to know then, just like today: how cheap does solar energy need to be to compete with fossil fuels? It might seem like a simple question, but there were so many things we didn't know that computer models were needed to figure out what the questions were, let alone give us answers. No models existed, so JPL needed to make them.

JPL had dozens of PhD economists, operations researchers, analysts, computer programmers, engineers, and scientists working on this problem.

Twenty of us were sitting around waiting for a conference call. A secretary popped her head in and said there was a call for Dr. Brun. He assumed it was the call we were waiting for and put it on the loudspeaker. The caller asked:

"Is this Dr. Brun?"

"Yes."

"Were you an engineering professor at UCLA?"

This was a strange question. We were expecting a call from a colleague in Washington to talk about some administrative stuff.

"Yes."

"Well, I'm Bill Watson and I'm the CEO of an advertising company in San Francisco. This might sound funny, but...next week is Secretary's Day, and the secretaries were looking through old copies of *Playgirl* magazine and voted you the man they most wanted to see jump out of a cake. Doctor, do you jump out of cakes?"

Twenty pairs of eyes turned slowly to Dr. Brun.

It turned out that, in addition to holding two PhDs and an MBA, he had been a centerfold in *Playgirl*. Some guys. As a friend once said, "It's not a talent pool; it's a talent puddle." Dr. Brun was in the puddle.

You might be interested to know that the financial model that came out of this work was the foundation for thousands of models which came later and resulted in hundreds of billions of dollars invested in alternative energy.

Chapter 9

Teaching: JPL Outreach

JPL encouraged its employees to teach and allowed flexibility in work hours to accommodate the many people at the lab who taught at local schools.

- - - - - - - - - -

Corona-Norco State Prison

I was teaching at a few places, including Corona-Norco State Prison, a medium-security prison east of Los Angeles that had a program to train the inmates to install solar energy systems. During the two-year program, they would learn the skills and get some experience so they hopefully could land a good-paying job when they got out.

Corona-Norco Prison was built after WWII from a military base given to the state by the army. The land and buildings had been owned by an Italian millionaire before the army commandeered them for the war effort. The millionaire's mansion had become the headquarters and cafeteria for the prison. The prison cafeteria was in a room that featured forty-foot painted ceilings and a fortune in grillwork.

The mansion also had a gold-plated swimming pool. *Corona-Norco Prison had, for real, a gold-plated swimming pool.*

The students in the solar installer class were a colorful group. To enter the program, an inmate needed to have at least two years left on his sentence, so none of the guys were choir boys. For example, I was showing a picture of long lines of cars waiting for gasoline during the 1973 Arab oil embargo, and one of the swarthier inmates asked me to stop. He walked over to the picture, pointed at a freeway underpass, and said, "That's where I used to buy my coke."

And when I mentioned that, as installers, they had to be careful what promises they made to the homeowner because their employer could be liable for these, he said:

> "I can say whatever I want; they'll never prove it."

You could see why this guy was in prison.

Another fellow was clearly smarter than all the other guys. I asked him where he had gone to school. He told me that he got his MBA at UCLA and his PhD in economics from the University of Southern California. I inquired:

"What the hell are you doing in here?"

He thought a moment, then said, "To be honest with you, I was running my business out of a briefcase, and it was snowing all the time."

A few weeks later, some of the first inmates were about to graduate from the program. One asked the instructor what happened to graduates. He told them that they would be sent to prisons that were installing solar systems to get some hands-on experience before being released. The inmate asked what prisons had installations going on. The instructor replied San Quentin and Soledad, which are maximum-security prisons with frequent brutal violence, in contrast to medium-security Corona-Norco with the gold-plated swimming pool.

A sudden chill swept across the room.

The inmate said, "Let me get this straight. When I graduate, you're going to transfer me from this nice medium-security prison to a war zone?"

The instructor affirmed this.

"I ain't graduating," said the inmate.

He walked from the room, and every single other inmate did the same. End of program. A little fender bender on the road to widespread solar energy.

Teaching At the Real Law School

I was also teaching alternative energy law at Whittier Law School, my alma mater, and one of my students missed the final. She claimed her husband had been diagnosed with a brain tumor the day before and she had to take care of the situation. I went to the dean to get permission to give her another final, and he said:

"Oh, did she use the brain tumor excuse again?"

Turned out it was the third straight semester she'd done this. A for creativity, F for redundancy!

- - - - - - - - - -

I had one assignment for the students that required them to speak to a businessperson in the solar industry, the gasoline station business, and a big oil or utility company. The one question they were required to ask was: "How often do you see a lawyer?"

The solar folks saw a lawyer once a year or so, to learn about new government incentives. The gas station people depended on the oil company lawyers. The oil company or utility executives spent over four hours a day with them.

The best lesson, though, came from the gas station operators who had been fined five thousand dollars per day for charging more than allowed for gasoline. They made twenty thousand dollars per day extra by charging more and would just cut a check for the five-thousand-dollar fine, no questions asked—needed to get out and do some more pumping.

Chapter 10

JPL General and Space Stories

These next stories don't have much to do with energy. JPL was mainly in the deep space business. Most of the lab was engrossed in the deep parts of space that only satellites could get to. Our energy work was a small part of JPL's work, and it seeped into the lab's consciousness only occasionally.

On the other hand, the space stuff was very cool— major-league toys, exquisite beauty, exotica. We always tried to get involved where we could. It was great fun and a nice vacation from the urgency of our energy and environmental work. The next few pages include some of the non-energy stories.

The Sex in Space Program

I love this story.

JPL got the assignment to design the conjugal bed for the International Space Station. Apparently, folks trying to join the two-hundred-mile-high club had a problem: when one person thrusts against another in space, they both go in the direction of the thrust until a wall gets in the way.

Volunteers for this "research and development" effort registered at an all-time high. Jacuzzis all over Pasadena were commandeered as simulated weightlessness conjugal test facilities that required careful scientific (and sometimes engineering) attention. That is my story and I'm sticking to it.

We interviewed a lot of people to get suggestions, and boy, did we get them. Velcro garters, bungee cords, padded rooms with handholds, fur handcuffs, giant clamshells, and something involving ice cube trays all received multiple endorsements. So much so that, after a while, we often ended interviews with comments like:

"Ya know, there's a guy (or girl) you should meet. You two have a lot in common."

It became a sort of dating service. At least one couple is still together, a happy little clamshell.

A PhD in "Kick It"

I heard on the radio one day that something was stuck on the *Voyager* spacecraft and threatened the whole mission. Then I heard on the radio that "JPL scientists had sent up new programming from the ground" and had solved the problem. I asked one of the *Voyager* scientists if he knew what the "new programming" was. He explained that something was stuck inside the satellite, so they programmed a camera arm to fully extend and then rebound to strike the satellite body right near the stuck part. This new genius science programming stuff was that *they kicked it*.

It's Raining

My first day on the job, I was in a van going to the JPL personnel office in the pouring rain. I remarked to the guy sitting next to me, "It's raining."

He asked, "Are you sure?"

I asked, "What else could it possibly be?"

He said, "Water falling from the sky."

I asked, "What do you do?"

He replied, "I'm the chief meteorologist for NASA."

I said, "You know too much; it's raining."

Uranus? Is There Another One?

Early that first day at JPL, I was at my desk when a brown-haired middle-aged man with a slight paunch and a leather jacket wheeled his bicycle into our room. He took off his leather jacket. Hung up his helmet. Kicked off his shoes. *Took off his pants* and hung them on a hook, and proceeded to sit cross-legged in his mighty-whitey underwear on one of the gray army surplus office chairs we used. He then pulled out a restaurant-sized *jar of peanut butter* and a *serving spoon*, took a big *shmear* of the peanut butter, stuck it in his mouth, finally noticed me taking in the show, burbled a hello through the gooey peanut mess in his mouth and started laughing. Rich Caputo and I have been friends ever since.

Because of Rich's sartorial business attire in flagrante, the typists (yes, we used typists back then, a now nearly extinct species vaguely related to the triceratops) would walk into our office backward to avoid looking at Rich's "fashion statement." Rich wrote speeches for the director of the lab, so the typists would come in waves to pick up changes and deliver drafts. They'd walk backward a few feet into the room, then hold the papers out behind them for Rich to take. Sometimes they'd just leave the papers at the door; then Rich would poke his head out, and, if the coast was clear, grab the papers and jump back in the room—fast.

Rich is crazy, talented, brilliant, nice, funny—a great mentor for me. He was also responsible for at least three extraordinary scientific and engineering masterpieces. The best had to do with the *Voyager* spacecraft, which is the first man-made object to have left the solar system, and after more than thirty years is still sending information back to earth. Although the *Voyager* was originally designed to run out of energy after passing Saturn (around four years), Rich and six others bootlegged the materials and modified the design so it would go for many decades, not just a few years. I personally think *Voyager* is one of the ten greatest engineering achievements of all time, certainly of the twentieth century, and Rich was one of the greats who made it happen.

The second masterpiece led to the largest natural gas finds in history. Rich noted that millions of years ago the earth's atmosphere was mostly natural gas, and asked:

"Where did all that gas go?"

Since the time that question was asked by Rich, we've found gas in coal and shale, trapped under lakes, and in thousands of places no one expected.

The third masterpiece was a very simple way of figuring how much of what we pay for energy, and even medical care, is "social costs."

When you do all that, I guess you don't have to wear pants if you don't want to.

Three months later, JPL had just successfully flown the *Voyager* spacecraft by Jupiter, and it was on its way to Saturn. Congress had that day authorized JPL to continue the *Voyager* mission for several more years. The new authorization was for something called the "Grand Tour," in which the spacecraft would travel past Uranus and Neptune before flying out of our solar system into interstellar space. This is what Rich and his cohorts were dreaming of when they bootlegged the nuclear battery. Man's first attempt to leave our solar system and communicate beyond it was made possible by not following orders. So American.

Bruce Murray, JPL's director, was worried about the press conference happening in the next hour, with live hookups to dozens of countries. He showed up at our door and said, "Rich, I can't go on television and tell five hundred million people that we're flying to Uranus [pronounced 'yer anus']. What do I do?!" Rich, with a sandwich's worth of peanut butter in his mouth, answered, "Call it Uranus [pronounced 'urine us']." Murray exclaimed, "That's a great idea; that's exactly what I'll do!" And that's what he did.

That night on NBC's national news broadcast, the sonorous anchor, Tom Brokaw, announced at the end of the program that NASA/JPL was flying to "urine us"; then he looked in the camera and cracked up.

- - - - - - - - - -

One of the coolest things about *Voyager* was the thick gold record secured to the side of the spacecraft. Pictographic instructions on how to assemble a player to listen to the sounds were engraved into a plaque alongside the gold record.

The record is truly one of the great assemblages of human sounds ever collected. It has superb examples of music from every corner of the globe, along with lovingly selected sounds of babies, heartbeats, trains, whales, and other samples. And in addition to these prime examples of our sonic world, leading off the record are fifty-five speeches from world leaders in their own languages.

Think about this a second. This is humankind's first organized attempt to leave our solar system and to tell unknowable but knowing organisms about ourselves. Billions have been spent, and the skill, hopes, and dreams of almost everyone on earth are riding in some ancient way on this thing. The eternal quest to reach out to other worlds. And the first thing this poor alien has to do is sort out fifty-five different languages?! I don't know about you, but my English is OK and I know a bit of Spanish and some tourist Thai—that's my max. I know a couple of people who speak six languages, but fifty-five?

On the side of the spacecraft are instructions for a RECORD PLAYER. *A record player*. Most people alive today have never seen or heard a record player, which have now been replaced by iPods and CD players, which didn't exist when *Voyager* was launched. And this record player has to play pictures, too. Dealt with RPMs on your record player lately? Maybe your grandfather did when he was a kid.

There are a few really funny things in those speeches, though. First of all, the recording starts with a few words from then Secretary-General of the United Nations, Kurt Waldheim. It later emerged that Waldheim was in fact a relic of the Nazis from World War II. So the first words this inhabitant of another world is going to hear will be spoken in heavily Austrian-accented English: "I send greetings on behalf of the pipple [people] of our planet." From a Nazi.

After a babble of a dozen or so languages, a voice comes on and says, like an emcee at a club in the New York Catskills, "HELLO, EXTRATERRESTRIALS." And then a little while later, another voice says: "As you probably already know, we are a question-mark-shaped country on the west coast of Africa."

"As you probably already know"? Can they see lines from space? Do they already know that Kurt Waldheim was a Nazi? What an interesting set of assumptions the speakers must have had.

The alien is going to need a space martini after listening to this thing. At least it'll have a record player.

I recently had a chance to go back to JPL and give a speech. Part of our job had been to predict the energy future twenty or thirty years hence. That was thirty-one years ago, so I had the chance to talk about what we'd gotten right and what we'd gotten wrong.

The best thing about the speech, though, was that a full-scale engineering replica of *Voyager* was right next to the podium, while the *Cassini* spacecraft flanked the other side of the stage. Both were wrapped in the shiniest gold foil you can imagine. A display about the sounds on the gold record was at the base of the stage stairs. That was so cool.

We'd definitely gotten some things right: the hybrid and electric car, oil prices, underground gasification, personal computers, even specific corruption and criminality. But we missed a few things too: the Internet and cell phones.

58

Lesson: everyone just has a batting average when it comes to predicting the future. I once made something like a hundred great decisions in a row—and then screwed up for the rest of the decade.

There Is a Solar System in My Oatmeal

I'm having breakfast one day in the JPL cafeteria and start chatting with some guy sitting next to me. We have the usual work conversation: "What do *you* do?" (Navigator for a future mission to Jupiter to be managed by JPL called Galileo.) "What do *you* do?" (Energy policy analysis.)

He explained to me that, because of the *Challenger* Space Shuttle crash and tragedy, solid fuels could no longer be used to power interplanetary space missions, but liquid fuels weren't powerful enough to get the spacecraft to Jupiter as in the earlier *Voyager* missions. They had no way to get their Galileo satellite to Jupiter.

I was eating oatmeal. He took it and smoothed out the surface, arranging raisins and walnuts to represent our solar system—"This walnut is the sun and this walnut is Jupiter, this small raisin is earth and this cube of sugar is Venus"—until he had the whole solar system in there. Then he started drawing lines in the oatmeal with his finger while withdrawing into his own thoughts. He drew some circles around raisin-earth and explained that you could go in fast orbits around earth and slingshot to Jupiter, but you still needed more energy than could be provided by liquid fuels. His slingshot mimicry sent oatmeal flying toward the big sun of a walnut, and he said, "The orbit's not big enough." Then he started musing to himself, "But you know, if we made the orbit all the way between Venus [sugar cube] and Earth [small raisin], we could build up enough energy to get to Jupiter!" He was drawing circles all over the cereal now, and oatmeal was flying everywhere, including on my shirt and his arms. He got really excited and ran from the table, leaving my oatmeal to congeal and the planets to drip off the table and onto my pants.

And believe it or not, that's exactly what they did. They called it "VEEGA," for Venus-Earth-Earth Gravity Assist. Galileo would slingshot once by Venus, and twice by Earth, gathering enough momentum to get to distant Jupiter. And it all started in my oatmeal.

Space has taken up enough space,

back to the energy stories...

Part 2

Sunlaw, My Sunlaw

Horse Ride (Arno Baernhoft)

Chapter 11

Background

Inventing Sunlaw

Sunlaw was the name of a company I started in 1980 when I left JPL as a full-time employee, but stayed on as a consultant. Sunlaw lasted for twenty-five years, drew on the lessons learned at JPL and was itself a pioneer, an explorer of alternative energy and environmental technology. I tried to borrow one particular thing from JPL—that any day at work something incredibly special could happen that could really, truly help the world.

Started with all the idealism and passion for energy independence and a clean environment that a child of the race to the moon and oil embargos could muster, I eventually found out that "pioneers get the arrows." Although the arrows ventilated me so I now can breathe through places not in God's blueprint, it was nevertheless a ride I was built for and cherished.

- - - - - - - - - -

The word "sunlaw" was the access code to the National Energy Legislative Database I worked on at JPL. A woman at the Franklin Research Institute came up with the word, and I thought she'd invented it. I had bought some license plates with "Sunlaw" on them. I started the company a year or two later, and I had the license plates, so I kept the name. I was traveling through Scotland sometime afterward and came across the Sunlaw House Hotel. It had been in continuous operation for over two hundred years, owned by the Sunlaw family, who changed their name to Roxborough in the 1700s. The family had existed for four or five hundred years before that.

So much for inventing a name.

It was a good one, though, because it reflected my focus on alternative energy and my training in law. Sunlaw.

The purpose of the company was to take advantage of the law I wrote about in both law school and JPL that permitted independent alternative energy companies to sell electricity to utilities. We had very little money—ten thousand dollars from a workers' compensation settlement (I had been a roofer after high school and a ladder broke). To support Sunlaw, I consulted for companies trying to create wind farms, giant solar electric power plants, waste-to-energy facilities, energy conservation programs, all kinds of things.

Having written the first law review article on this new alternative energy law, as well as a book on its regulations, and having given countless speeches, I was sought after by companies that wanted help with selling power to electric utilities, and by utilities that wanted help negotiating when buying power from alternative energy producers.

For example, a paper company hired me to negotiate a contract for its new cogeneration power plant. It mainly made toilet paper; one of those ultra-soft, makes your ass feel like it's wrapped in fur kind of toilet papers. We passed by a warehouse with hundreds of gigantic, brightly colored rolls of this toilet paper, each as tall as a pro basketball player and wider than the free-throw lane. Apparently, the little tiny baby rolls we actually use were cut from these roll-zillas. I mean, there were millions and millions of rolls in this one room. And it struck me like lightning: *Could there be that much s—t, and that many a—holes in the world?* For the first time, I got a sense of just how big the world really is, and that there is indeed a glut of a—holes.

Another time, a company from Israel, Ormat Turbine, had built a prototype of something called a solar pond. A solar pond is a way of making electricity from the sun using a gigantic swimming pool. Hot salt water at the bottom of the pond is covered by cold fresh water that holds the heat in. A special electric generator that works at these relatively low temperatures extracts the heat as electricity. The company wanted to sell electricity to Southern California Edison and hired me to assist it.

At that time the price of oil, which drove the price of electricity back then, had finally come down after being in the stratosphere for a long time. The high oil prices had caused a recession and bad economic times.

The Saudi oil minister had tried to warn OPEC that keeping the price high encourages oil's competitors— like Ormat for renewable energy, but also natural gas, coal, and nuclear power providers.

The Minister from Saudi Arabia told OPEC, "The stone age didn't end because they ran out of stones."

Solar energy is and was expensive, so Ormat needed some pretty high prices to make its system profitable. Justified when oil and electricity prices were really high, the system was uneconomic at more moderate prices.

Southern California Edison representatives talked about how to make the economics work for everybody, whether prices were low, as they were on that day, or high, as they are when there is trouble in the Middle East and the OPEC producers use oil as a weapon against the West.

The Israeli project manager from Ormat looked at the SCE executive and observed:

"You vant the bad [Middle East disruption] scenario? I can guarantee it."

Everybody laughed and Ormat got its contract. The Middle East—it's a laugh riot.

Transition to Building Plants

Solar ponds are just one example. We worked on climate change, urban air pollution, alternative fuels, many solar electricity systems, waste-to-energy, catalytic converters, smart grid, greenhouse gases, and just about every other form of alternative energy and pollution control device out there.

In addition to this consulting or project management stuff, Sunlaw also developed, owned, and operated two of the first cogeneration power plants in the United States, and probably the world. To do this, we needed eighty-six million dollars; I tell that story a little later in the book.

We eventually raised the money and built our plants in a town called Vernon. Vernon is a small, exclusively industrial area just south of downtown Los Angeles and just east of the University of Southern California (USC).

Aztec Princess (Eloy Torrez) Power Plant by Bob
Danziger

This picture was originally posed to be the cover of my
second CD, *Where Pirates Roam*. It is now in use as
the cover for one of my four iTunes albums, *One Rock*.
That's my power plant behind me—the *Aztec Princess*
mural is painted on the back of the control room.
That's me in the middle, and over my shoulder you can
see the box that the jet engine that made our electricity
is in. Notice the railroad tracks and weeds between me
and the camera.

70

Taken at a time when Sunlaw and I had survived some deep lows, this picture represents the artistic, musical, engineering, environmental, community, and business successes achieved against staggering odds.

The LM Fraternity

The vice president for Ecomagination at General Electric calls the people who were the drivers of this energy efficiency and alternative energy world the "LM Fraternity." Sunlaw was a big part of that fraternity. The LM Fraternity is not at all well-known, yet is responsible for more energy conservation (over one billion barrels of oil and counting) and more greenhouse gas reductions (over two billion tons and counting) than any other set of events or groups in human history. The amount of alternative energy implemented by this fraternity is equivalent to all the power generation in the United States (one "U.S. equivalent"). LM stands for "Land and Marine," a part of General Electric that adapted jet engines for power generation.

My power plant was the first. We kept our promise to the *Aztec Princess*.

In 2008, for the first time, investment in renewables was 5 percent greater than in fossil fuels. Of over two hundred fifty billion dollars invested in new power sources, more than half went to renewables for the first time. Much of this accomplishment is owed to the PURPA law, which made non-utility ownership of power plants possible, and to the LM Fraternity, which made it a worldwide success. Bad things happened too, like Enron, but that side of the story is for a different book.

Perhaps the most significant part of the LM Fraternity story is that it is one example of an idea going from concept to massive worldwide implementation. Any new energy or environmental technology that is going to make a difference will have to do something on this scale or larger.

Dad: The American Dream

My father grew up very poor and sold newspapers on the corner of Randolph and Clark in Chicago. He came from circumstances so adverse that it's a miracle he visited so little of that trauma on my sister and me. As a six-year-old, he had to walk to his job in the snow, and the family was dependent on his earnings to eat. The real thing.

Almost sixty years later, I stood in a conference room on the twenty-third floor of a bank building on that very corner, signing for a loan of several tens of millions of dollars for the first "project financed" independent power projects. These projects were the first of the hundreds of LM Fraternity projects worldwide that have saved billions of barrels of oil and avoided tons of pollution. The American Dream, indeed.

There were some funny things that happened, but this was so special I'll just leave it here.

Chapter 12

Develop, Finance

Dead Wouldn't Hurt

Sunlaw was required to take out a fifteen-million-dollar life insurance policy on me at a time when we were hurting for money, making me worth far more dead than alive. The law required that if I were to die the company still had to have enough money on hand to protect investors.

I tried just promising not to die, but the bankers didn't go for it.

Sunlaw raised some money to buy a fifteen-million-dollar life insurance policy on me. I had no money or savings, owned no real estate or cars, and owed almost two million dollars.

The company was in a fix and needed money. Everyone was really worried about where we were going to raise more money, and discussions were going on all the time. Every now and then I'd see the vice presidents talking down the hall, and slowly, very slowly, all of them would turn and look at me. I could just hear them thinking, *Fifteen million dollars would come in real handy right now, hmm?*

To them, I was worth far more dead than alive. Not a good feeling. I'm glad we got the projects financed—just in the nick of time.

TOSCO

A company called TOSCO—which stands for The Oil Shale Corporation—wanted to buy Sunlaw. TOSCO had a chunk of oil shale the size of an SUV in the lobby of its twentieth-floor offices in Century City, near Los Angeles. Someone was smoking and tried to put out a cigarette on the giant rock, lighting it instead and causing quite a unique situation for firefighters. Rumor has it that the rock burned its way through five floors before they finally put it out.

TOSCO wanted to use its stock to buy us. I asked the company representatives what they would do if oil prices fell. Their VP of Strategic Planning looked at me and declared, "But the price of oil can't go down." I looked at him and said, "We'll take cash." Right then, the telephone rang; a TOSCO person answered it, looked over at me, and announced, "Destiny calling."

Destiny was the first name of my executive assistant. Destiny calling indeed.

Deal over. One month later, oil started dropping until it had fallen by almost 80 percent, and then it stayed at that low price for over fifteen years. TOSCO stock dropped more than 90 percent.

Let's Put the Chicken Back In

The story that takes the lawyer cake for me happened later, when one of our outside attorneys and two of his colleagues came by the office for a lunch meeting. A tall strapping lawyer-person got some chicken sandwich stuck in his throat and started choking. His associate, a petite woman, attempted the Heimlich maneuver, but he was too big and she was too short. He was turning blue. I ran over behind him and give him a quick bear hug. A piece of chicken flew out of his mouth and across the room, and he lay down panting and catching his breath. "You saved me," he croaked, and expressed much gratitude.

Then, he went back to his office and *billed me* for the time he spent while I was saving his life, and shortly after that he quit the law firm and went to work elsewhere. I saw him a few weeks later and asked him about it, and he just thought it was the funniest thing he'd ever done. I was thinking, *I get to put the chicken back in, don't I?*

Water, Please?

The bankers and lawyers working with our company were doing something called "due diligence," which is when they try to find the flaws and problems in a project. It's sort of a financial colonoscopy. This is something AIG forgot to do so far this millennium, but only on projects that could bring down the whole financial system.

The bankers had hired the managing partner of the biggest law firm in the United States to represent them. He and the bankers were in a conference room, questioning us and exploring what we would do with the steam we were making if our customer went out of business. "Could we truck the steam away?" they asked. This may not sound funny or stupid to you, but trust me, ask an engineer and he or she will howl. I responded, "We could condense the steam [make it back into water] at our site and truck it to another site and reheat it [i.e., turn it back into steam again]." They thought it a good answer—but it was a joke.

Trust me, this is funny.

Everything but War, Civil War, and Atomic Explosion

The essence of project financing is covering all the risks and getting a party to undertake liability for the risks that it controls. It's like getting a big department store to sign a lease before building a mall. Add some extended warranties on steroids, throw in a few fancy insurance policies, and presto—you've got a power plant.

This is risk allocation, project finance style. But even if all contractors and owners and government agencies and so on involved in one of these financings took liability for everything in their control, there are still gaps and overlaps and things beyond the control of all. That's where insurance comes in, or at least it used to.

At the time we went to Lloyd's of London, our lenders had a list of risks and issues that weren't covered by any of the other contracts. An insurance policy of this type had never been done before, certainly not for alternative energy, so there was a lot of uncertainty about where we were going to come out.

Negotiating for Lloyd's was a Mr. Nottage, a very serious man with an encyclopedic mind and a big black patch over one eye.   Mr. Nottage was one of two specialty brokers who organized policies for things like the Olympics, hurricanes, earthquakes, and Betty Grable's legs.

After several days of negotiating, we reached an agreement. Lloyd's offered a policy that would cover everything but war, civil war, and atomic explosion.

Everyone was thrilled. I called our lead banker at First Chicago and explained our great success. He asked me, dead seriously:

> "Well, what do you intend to do about those?"

> "Do about what?" I replied.

> "War, civil war, and atomic explosion."

I looked at the phone like this guy was from Mars. I couldn't believe the guy wanted me to find a way to solve war, civil war, and atomic explosions.

I was over-rated.

- - - - - - - - - -

More sensible heads were studying an alternative energy system for Sunnyvale Air Force Station. Security was exceptionally tight, and the walls of the room that needed heating and cooling were made of six-foot-thick reinforced concrete. I asked the officer what the chances were that Sunnyvale would close. He answered, "The only way this base is closing is if there is a successful nuclear attack on North America, and then you don't give a damn, now do you?"

I finally replied to Mr. First Chicago and, in one of those instances when you think of the right line at the right time instead of a year later, said, "We could develop our own first-strike capability, but that would probably cause a significant cost overrun." Mr. First Chicago said, "OK."

I went back to visit with Mr. Nottage and finalize some details. On breaks during the negotiations, I played a small music synthesizer, fooling around with bass lines or playing the melody of people's voices. Mr. Nottage led me to a balcony above the trading floor and Lloyd's famous bell from the first insured shipwreck, took out his own keyboard, and we jammed quietly behind the balustrade.

Extended Warranties on Steroids

My favorite story about extended warranties happened at a meeting of all the people who used the kind of General Electric engine we did. While we were using it for power generation, others used it on airplanes (Boeing 747, C5-A), ships (destroyers and ferries), and other big stuff. What I hadn't known is that the aircraft version of the engine was also used in cruise missiles. Yes, cruise missiles. Bombs that fly themselves.

We had been discussing the details of extended warranties and extolling their importance, hoping to get GE to improve the terms. The cruise missile guys looked a little confused, so I stopped and asked if they had a question.

The missile guy replied, "We don't care about warranties. We want it to blow up."

Palms I and II – Ask Him About Feet

As I mentioned, First Chicago is the bank that originally proposed to finance our power plants, although it had financial trouble in the middle of the deal and we had to restart a few months later. While things were still hot and heavy, the bank's representative in Los Angeles, a nice woman in her forties, invited me to dinner in order to learn more about the Sunlaw projects and the company in general.

We agreed to meet at the Palm Restaurant on Santa Monica Boulevard, near Doheny, the border between Hollywood and Beverly Hills. At least that's where I was, and early, as usual. She was ten minutes late, then twenty, finally thirty, so I called her office. She answered, fuming mad at me. "How dare you...!" sputter, sputter, etc. "You weren't there, and even if you were there...!" sputter, sputter. She was pissed off.

I said, "Hold on. I've been here since five thirty and I haven't seen you at all." She fumed, "Well, I was there and you weren't there." I told her I was the only customer; she couldn't have missed me.

Then I remembered that in New York there is a Palm Restaurant on Second and Forty-fifth, and right across the street is a sister restaurant called Palm Too. I asked the banker lady if she was at the Palm near Doheny, and Beverly Hills. No. It turned out she was at the Palm near La Cienega, and it wasn't a restaurant, it was a bar.

I convinced her there was some mistake and that she should come to the Palm near Doheny. After we got off the phone, I asked the maître d' if there was another Palm nearby, like in New York. He told me no, but over near La Cienega there was a *heavy leather S&M lesbian bar* called something like Palm's.

Oops.

- - - - - - - - - -

Eventually, First Chicago opted out of the deal, but not because of the leather lesbian bar thing. However, one upshot of First Chicago not doing our project was that one banker got it in his head that we owed the bank some money for its decision to leave the deal. He would come out to our offices and ask for the money, and we would politely decline, and then he'd come out again a few months later; we went through this dance for a year or so. At this point, he started getting a little belligerent, and one of my assistants, a very beautiful and nice lady, who had been stuck with this guy in an elevator for a couple of hours when the power went out, told me, "Ask him about feet." She would not explain.

Next time he called, I asked, "Seen any nice feet lately?" And we never heard from him again.

Bayoneting the Wounded

One thing about being the first to raise more than eighty-six million dollars for a brand-new company—with inexperienced management and no capital whatsoever, in an entirely new industry, using an entirely new financing technique, in a very high-profile situation—is that the investors, lawyers, and accountants get pretty much whatever they want.

Our negotiating position was, shall we say, flexible.

Some of the things they wanted were quarterly audits and monthly certified reports. Most companies only get an annual audit and a few other modest controls. Our leash was tight.

This actually was completely fine with me because my father was an auditor, so I knew what was expected. We just played it totally straight and kept good records. We were also fortunate to be very profitable; we could pay our taxes and still make a great return to our investors.

Not everyone in alternative energy was so honest. There was a loophole in the law (nonrecourse debt) that allowed some crooked developers to make great profits from the tax loophole, and they put in shoddy windmills that wouldn't have made a profit even if they had run. The IRS found them out, with the fraud division clawing back the taxes and a few going to jail. Very Enron.

After making its way through some dubious wind and solar projects, the IRS fraud division turned to Sunlaw. Sunlaw had worked on something called cogeneration, also known as combined heat and power. The power plants made their electricity with special jet engines, and the hot air that came out of the back of the engines was used to make refrigeration, like the gas refrigerators in motor homes. The IRS wanted to know if we were a scam also.

We'd been audited every three months, and cheating was impossible. All of this was done by KPMG, one of the largest accounting firms in the world. We were so clean.

Anyway, the IRS went over us with a fine-tooth comb. After several months, the lead agent met with us at our offices, looked me in the eye, shook my hand, and said, "You actually paid taxes." He nodded his head in approval, and while walking out the door, said:

"Normally, it's the auditor's job to bayonet the wounded."

Chapter 13

See Your Two Swiss and Raise You One Jew

Sunlaw sought to eliminate its emissions and did several hundred experiments with GE and others to accomplish this. Eventually, we were introduced to a company called Advanced Catalyst Systems, and we started inventing and co-developing together, forming a company called Goal Line Environmental Technologies. This resulted in the most advanced air pollution control technology for power plants and made our power plant the cleanest in the world.

In addition to making the technology ourselves, we sold a license on the patents. ABB, a company based in Switzerland, licensed the patents from us and owed us the million-dollar up-front fee. The money didn't show up, and I was bugging Bob, my contact. We needed the money badly. Time went on and frustrations were mounting. I had to start being a little threatening, although we had no money to pay lawyers to sue these guys.

Finally, Bob called me and said that before they paid us, two officials from Swiss headquarters wanted to come out and talk to me. A meeting was arranged for three days later, and these two guys from Zurich showed up.

They explained to me that Switzerland was a nation of bankers—bankers that don't give money out, but take money in and keep it safe. So what they wanted to do was proceed with the contract and take the technology, with only one small change: they wouldn't pay us. That's right, everything exactly the same, except we wouldn't get paid.

In another one of those rare moments of having the right line at the right time (instead of a year later), I looked at them and countered, "I'll see your two Swiss and raise you one Jew; give me the money."

They didn't say another word—just got up, handed me our check, and flew back to Switzerland.

Chapter 14

Just Checking His Emissions, Claims Official

As a power plant owner, I spent a lot of my time with government agencies like those that govern air quality.

I had started dating a woman who was an official with a government air-regulating agency. Things were going well when she called me to break off the relationship. She told me she'd had a dream in which she opened up the newspaper over her morning coffee and the headline read: "Air Quality Official Sleeping with Major Polluter; Just Checking His Emissions, Claims Official."

Chapter 15

"Who?!?"

The Story of Winning the New York Film Festival Gold Medal for Best Original Music

It may sound strange but I thought of my energy company as a sculpture, actually conceptual art, and we did many unusual things for an energy company. Among these was filming the building of the power plants in time lapse, along with other footage. Many of the workers at the site had never been able to show their families what they did—the building sites were often far from home and pretty dangerous places for a kid. We thought that if we could give all of them a video that they could take home and show their families, maybe they would work just a little bit better and safer. Since it was a union site, we gave control of the cameras to the union guys so they didn't think we were using the cameras to spy on them. We collected all kinds of stills and video.

The principal photographer became pregnant not long after the two-year construction period commenced. She insisted on going up the ladder to the roof to check on the time-lapse camera and to take some stills. These hard-bitten steelworkers' union guys and gals, who regularly risked their lives under tons of equipment, would absolutely quail with fear when she went up that ladder. They'd offer to help, beg to help, but Mary would have none of it. Eventually, when she was further along in the pregnancy, she had no choice and accepted their help. I grew to like those folks a lot.

I had to review all of the footage and stuff as part of assembling the video. It turned out that we had some good footage, and we also had sixteen hours of concrete drying. I watched all sixteen of those hours to extract the maybe thirty seconds of good footage sandwiched between that decreasingly wet concrete.

The cinematic value of sixteen hours of concrete drying has rarely been as thoroughly explored.

With Tee Bosustow producing the video (son of the man responsible for *Mr. Magoo*), I did the music and sound effects for the finished product, using very early and primitive digital recording gear. Unbeknownst to me, Tee submitted the video (about fourteen minutes in its final form) to the New York Film Festival for consideration.

Much to everyone's surprise I got a nomination for Best Original Music.

I was trying to decide if it was worth the time and money to fly to New York from Los Angeles for the big awards dinner. I asked Tee if it was a real award, or some fake thing that might be used by a producer to make his client feel good, something that is fairly common for political consultants to do. He assured me that it was a real award from a recognized peer-selected film festival with tens of thousands of submittals from dozens of countries. He explained that gold, silver, and bronze medals were given in each category, and there could be up to seven honorable mentions as well.

I felt I didn't want to spend the money to go to New York just to be an also-ran, and I was up against some of the great composers in film. Even though the category I was in included the music from documentaries, industrial films, commercials, and television shows—more or less everything but feature films—big composers like John Williams and Elmer Bernstein were also nominated.

Tee decided to call the festival to see if he could find out if I'd won a medal or something—and trust me, we didn't think I had. He got someone from the festival on the phone and explained our situation. After a bit, she came back on the line and said that I definitely should come to New York. Tee then took a shot and told the woman that if it was only the silver or bronze medal, we might not go. She hemmed and hawed for a minute and declared again that we definitely should come to New York, that I had "won a real good one." Then she broke down, explaining that they needed some music from the winner for the ceremony and could we please send some in.

I'd won the gold medal! When my mom, who's a very good musician, heard who the other nominees were, she was convinced they had made a mistake. She may have been right; I'm good, but not nearly in their league. It might have been that it was the festival's first all-digital submission, or the way I used industrial sounds. I don't know. I do know John Williams is a lot better than I am, but I was still thrilled to win.

On the other hand, I'm guessing that I'm the only recipient of a gold medal for Best Original Music who also conceived an industry, invented key technology, did a first-of-a-kind project financing that was copied enough to build a whole United States of power plants, was the first to eliminate an entire class of pollutants from a working power plant, and re-wrote the record books for power plant performance that resulted in the largest energy conservation and greenhouse gas reduction event in history (to date). Just guessing.

The Best Original Music category came about an hour into the program. Fifteen hundred people in the Sheraton ballroom; eating, applauding, milling, listening, hoping, stricken, etc. But the judges did not award a gold medal for best original music to a feature film. A murmur ran through the crowd. The judges had the discretion to refrain from awarding a medal in a given category, but until then, no medals had been omitted. I got real nervous.

Then they started my category, describing the work of each of the seven honorable mentions, the bronze winner, and the silver. Then, "The winner of the gold medal for Best Original Music in a Short Film is…Bob Danziger." And everyone in the audience, as one, looked up and said:

"Who?"

~

~

Chapter 16

If Only Animals Could Buy Records

Just after Thanksgiving every year, my friend Joe invites me to his ranch in the Texas hill country. Originally, I came for a deer hunt, but after a few years I'd bring my kalimba instead of a gun, to see if I could get the deer to dance. The kalimba is a small African instrument sometimes called a "thumb piano."

I'd often played and whistled for birds because sometimes I could catch their attention and get them to respond. I'd learned how to do that from Cecil Taylor, who told me to go to the banks of the Delaware River and learn rhythm from the birds.

The deer dancing started when I had gotten out of my stand to wait for a ride back to the ranch house. I was fooling around on the kalimba, looked up, and there was a young four-point buck not twenty feet away, staring at me. Though deer normally spook easily, the sound of the kalimba somehow soothed his instinct to flee.

I played the kalimba a bit and he snorted. I tried to be as still as I could, looking down at the kalimba, then sneaking a glance at the deer. I launched into an improvised song in a loping rhythm, and the deer took about four steps to the right, stopped, and snorted. I kept playing. The deer took about eight steps to the left, stopped, and snorted. Sort of a venison line dance. This went on for three or four minutes until the truck drove up and the deer bounded away.

I told my hosts about it, and they had visions of me leading a chorus line of deer dancing like the Rockettes at Radio City Music Hall. And in fact, in the bars around town, the legend grew from one or two deer to whole herds of 'em doing synchronized routines with all kinds of fancy moves. They didn't believe me because, well, let's just say, a tall tale or two got told on these outings.

I was hooked. Now my "hunt" was to see if I could get the deer to dance. I would sit in the blind in the dark of the early morning, waiting for the sun to come up and the deer to stir. Then, when they made their appearance, I would play the kalimba, using the deer's footfalls as my rhythm. After a while, I would alter the rhythm and many of the deer changed their movement to reflect the new rhythm.

I decided to go over to Joe's cousin's ranch, where he was breeding thoroughbred horses. Around Christmastime he weaned the foals from their mothers and all were pretty upset. I thought playing for the horses might calm them down a little, so I went into the corral where the foals were, played for them, and they settled right down. One or two put their heads over my shoulders to listen and nibble at the kalimba, those big brown eyes and sweet, sweet hearts connecting with me and the music.

Then I went into the eighty-acre field, head down and shoulders hunched, and walked backward toward the mares while playing the kalimba. After running around the field for a while, eventually the mares gathered around until curiosity got the better of a few and they would come up behind me, often two at a time, and put their heads over my shoulders, listening and trying to nibble the kalimba, just like the babies.

That's how I got hooked on playing for animals, and I started taking my kalimba to zoos and other places animals might be found. I ended up playing at an Australian wild animal park for a platypus (not so interested), a Tasmanian devil (wild spinning and yelping—definitely more of a heavy metal kind of animal), and koala bears.

For those of you who don't know, the koala bear is a perpetually stoned animal that eats only the hallucinogenic leaves of certain eucalyptus trees. They rest in the crotches of the trees, mostly so they don't fall out due to being high. I was standing next to their keeper and playing for them. One young koala very slowly turned his head toward me and very...very slowly sort of raised an eyebrow. The keeper exclaimed, "Wow, he LOVED it!" I guess that's rockin' the house, koala-style.

Chapter 17

Supertramp

While running Sunlaw I'd done several studio albums, but really wanted to play live and find out what I could do in front of an audience. I formed a band for a year or so. I wrote the music, sang lead, and played the kalimba. Although the kalimba is mainly an African instrument, versions of it appear in cultures all over the world because of its simplicity of construction—it's made from a slab of wood and strips of springy metal.

I originally bought the kalimba for a hike and camping trip because it was small and seemed rugged. It was OK to play, but nothing special, and after a while it was way out of tune, but I kept it in my luggage. I was passing through Charles De Gaulle Airport in Paris on my way to Milan, and there was a Steinway grand piano on a pedestal in the middle of the international terminal being worked on by a piano tuner. I showed him the kalimba.

He tuned it to a pentatonic scale—the scale that makes every note you hit sound pretty. Basically, he put magic in it, and every time I touched it something beautiful —at least to me— happened, and I began carrying it all over the world with me.

The next magic happened when I was wandering around southern Thailand, playing the kalimba and a small battery-powered synthesizer in walks through the jungle and on visits to small islands. Had to be careful, though—on one island near Phang Nga a woman became quite mesmerized by the music, and her husband tried to give her to me! With seven wives, he could spare one, but not my thing. Not enough teeth.

When my guide took me on walks through the jungle, children would appear out of nowhere. With no TV, newspapers, and little schooling, they had never seen anything like me before—a giant white guy walking through the jungle playing an African instrument and a synthesizer.

As we were wandering, playing for the kids and watching them play, my right thumb started moving in a way that made a nice steady beat and played a pretty chord that set up the left thumb to do a melody. This gave me something special on the kalimba, and it became my favorite instrument, drawing me away from the bass guitar and into voice, percussion, and other kinds of instruments and music.

- - - - - - - - - -

Three people in my band primarily played with a group called Supertramp. They were recording what was to become the album *Some Things Never Change*, and Rick Davies wanted to put some kalimba on the first song. They called me and asked if I was familiar with Supertramp's music, which I said I was, and actually was by the next Tuesday, when they had me come in with my kalimbas to do some recording. Bass kalimbas, soprano kalimbas, hand-wrought or machine-made, every kalimba I owned was tuned and ready for the session.

The bass kalimba was a bit of a miracle because it was out of tune with itself (overtones) due to its shape. They had specifically asked for a bass kalimba, so in desperation I just got out the jigsaw and cut odd-shaped holes on either side of this big box. Somehow, some way, it worked, and the bass was dead-on.

The session went pretty well, and they included several passages in the final song. I was thrilled—a CEO of an energy company and more or less amateur musician being included on a real album based on merit! So it was very special that I was able to be in London on business when Supertramp was launching its European tour at Royal Albert Hall—the Carnegie Hall of Great Britain.

They let me play on the stage during sound check, which was cool, but told me that even though I had a backstage pass, I had to be in my seat for the opening of the show and could come back after the second song. I protested, but they insisted, and my friends in the band smiled as they shooed me up to my seat.

I was in my seat, sitting next to strangers, when the lights dimmed and then went out. The crowd started to roar, and over the giant loudspeakers came a recording of something I had played in the kalimba recording session, but wasn't on the album. I think it was about a minute or two of the same kalimba that was tuned in the Paris airport.

I was thrilled, just overjoyed. This was my Carnegie Hall moment, as small as it might be. The crowd was going nuts; the curtains drew back, the lights came up, and there was the band, just as a recording of my bass kalimba joined Cliff Hugo on the electric bass and put a major thump on Royal Albert Hall.

I could barely contain myself—thirty years of work and this was likely the biggest stage I would ever experience. I said to the lady sitting next to me, "That's me playing!" She crossed her arms, gave me the wary, disgusted, are-you-crazy look, and retorted:

"Yeah, sure, buddy, that's why we're sitting out here. I'm the piano player."

Chapter 18

Record Profits

I never did make a profitable career out of music, despite the award, although it's been a happy and balancing part of my life. I kind of got close a couple of times, and in particular had the opportunity to record some CDs of my own music, take some singing lessons that were great fun, and play with extremely talented and funny musicians. I have five albums on iTunes and earn around two hundred dollars a year from sales. Other royalties alone sometimes bring in about two dollars per year, and most statements show less income than the cost of the stamp.

Part 3

The Community

Chapter 19

Vernon and Vernon Elementary School

It is not well-known how charitable public utilities tend to be. With a reach into every corner of a city, they often know what's really going on in ways that the police, politicians, and social workers never could. In addition, one finds a very high percentage of nice, solid people at utilities, the kind of people one would be delighted to have as a neighbor.

There is high personal motivation for utility people to help their communities, and the public utility commissions cooperate by encouraging the utilities to spend reasonable amounts of ratepayer's money to help out where they can.

As a result, when I came into this business, there was a long tradition of community involvement in the best sense of the words. I personally felt the same way, as did my investors, and from JPL I certainly learned about some good things we could do. The fact that we were profitable definitely helped, but mostly we were happy to be part of this tradition.

- - - - - - - - - -

I built my power plants in an industrial area next to the mean streets of Los Angeles. Gangs, drugs, and the homeless oozed between the factories, families, and working people of all kinds. It was real life. I drove through an area thick with homeless every day to get to my office; it's the same area seen in the movie *The Soloist*, starring Jamie Foxx and Robert Downey, Jr.

The city of Vernon was our home, and its motto "Exclusively Industrial" belied a town rich in family tradition, with ninety-six inhabitants to be exact. All residents lived in city housing and had city jobs. Founded in the early 1900s, Vernon did not have a contested election for mayor or city council until 2006. For many years, the city didn't even have an election because none of the incumbents had a challenger.

The city manager was the highest-paid official in the United States, with big Cadillacs and SUVs provided at city expense. And he was pretty much worth it— running a two-hundred-seventy-million-dollar surplus from the city's electric utility and litigation victories, which provided a net surplus of almost three million dollars per resident. Rent for city housing was eighty-five dollars a month.

Site of one of the rare double-knockouts in championship boxing history, LA weatherman Fritz Coleman thought Vernon's motto should be "It's not Club Med, but it's not dead." For the "not dead" part, he was pointing at weeds growing between the cracks in the sidewalk in front of leaking barrels of toxic waste.

Supported by the firefighters' union, a fire captain challenged the mayor and campaigned hard. He came home after a shift at the fire station to find that his house had been bulldozed. Three envelopes were nailed to poles stuck in the ground where his living room used to be. The first envelope contained a letter telling him that he had been fired from his position as fire captain. The second letter evicted him from his city-owned house; he was no longer eligible to live in the house because he'd been fired. The third envelope held a notice that he was disqualified to run for mayor because he no longer lived in the city.

The irony is that several years later the mayor was arrested for claiming he lived in Vernon, in an office building next to his restaurant (the only restaurant in the area with liquor license, because after his was granted the city council voted to prohibit any more liquor licenses). It turned out the police thought his "vacation" home ten miles away in a fancy part of Los Angeles, where his family lived and where he spent 90 percent of his time, should be considered his main residence.

- - - - - - - - -

The actual and alleged shenanigans of Vernon go back to its founding as a place for farm workers to work when harvest time was over. But for all its Chicago-machine-cum-western-gunslinger vibe, there were still children who went to Vernon Elementary School across the street from the city hall, with a factory that made pumps for nuclear power plants on one side and a Catholic church for the deaf on the other. All day, four hundred large diesel trucks passed by the school per hour, on the way to the other factories in the area.

- - - - - - - - - -

Along with the 270 students from mostly working-poor Hispanic families living in surrounding cities, the school also educated migrant farm worker children during the off-season. The least-funded school in the Los Angeles Unified School District, it sits in the dirtiest ZIP code in the United States because of the trucks and factories.

With all that, one wouldn't expect much, yet the school had double the average reading and math scores for LA elementary schools. Teachers, staff, and parents put their hearts and souls into this school, and the local business community helped where it could. The company that adopted the school before we did was one that made bikinis.

We helped by sponsoring assemblies and field trips, buying supplies and science programs for the teachers, and establishing a library. Career Days were big events because speakers from all over the world came to little Vernon to share their thoughts and encourage the kids. An art contest led to a mural program. You can see some of their work and other murals at the power plants at EnergyLaughs.com.

We were having an assembly in late June and the temperature was well over one hundred degrees. The design of the school—few windows, boxy structures, and southern exposure—made the classrooms into solar collectors, increasing the temperature to suffocating levels. The four hundred large diesel trucks that passed by the school every hour spewed all sorts of contaminants in the air that made breathing dangerous and learning almost impossible. And yet, double the average reading and math scores. The staff members were magicians.

We made a commitment to try to get the school some air-conditioning. Sears agreed to contribute the equipment, the union workers agreed to supply free labor, the electric utility agreed to provide free electricity, and we agreed to do and pay for everything the others weren't contributing. We were stopped cold by some bureaucratic hoo-ha. A real head shaker.

As a stopgap measure, I proposed at least getting fans for each room, but the principal explained that they couldn't accept just any fan. It had to have a tight cage so students didn't put their fingers—or worse—into the path of the blades. Noise was a factor, too; the fan couldn't be so noisy that the teacher was inaudible. The principal persuaded us that ordering the fans through the school district was the only option.

So we ordered three dozen fans through the school district and paid for them.

Two years later, a single hurricane fan showed up at the school, with gaps in the cage literally big enough to put a child's head through. When you turned it on, it was so loud that it was hard to hear even with people shouting, and the single speed of the fan was so powerful that any papers in were swept up and blown around the room like in a tornado—which is what the fan was designed to do on a Hollywood set.

Finally, I'd had enough. Working through the school district was accomplishing nothing. From then on, whenever the school needed something, the item just showed up. Ten computers? Look on the front steps; there they are. Two hundred student chairs? On the front lawn. Three dozen quiet fans with tight grills? In the entryway.

And the students made me my most precious possession: a book they wrote and illustrated entitled *All About Mr. Danziger*.
Veronica said, "I like Mr. Danziger because when he comes to our school he always makes a lot of noise with us."

The kids favorite, though, was the fact that my Dad worked for me. They thought the idea of being the boss of your father was just fantastic. Jeannette writes in their book, "Mr. Danziger enjoys being president because his father retired and he hired his dad. Now he gets to be the boss of his father, and tell his dad what to do. He says, "It is good to be your dad's boss."'

My dad did work for me after he retired, but he didn't take orders well. Generally, I asked what he wanted to do and then he went and did it, just like you'd expect a dad who was his own boss for fifty years to do. But the kids just loved the idea of being able to boss around your dad.

Chapter 20

102 Years

A local radio station selected me as "Citizen of the Week" for my work with the City of Hope Medical Center and Vernon Elementary School.

And what a group of honorees they were. One U.S. Marine while on his honeymoon went on a narrow ledge outside his third-story room and caught a baby that had fallen from the tenth floor. Another fellow saved an elderly woman from a man beating her with a pipe.

Sitting next to me was a 102-year-old woman who had helped found Alcoholics Anonymous. When it was her turn to be introduced, the host asked what her secret to longevity was.

"Old whiskey and young men," she replied.

I asked her if she had any problems at her age, and she told me that when dating now, she encountered a generation gap, or two, or three.

And then she told us the story of the 114-year-old man who had recently died. She noted that he had smoked cigars until he was ninety-six, and that his doctor said that if he'd stopped smoking thirty years earlier, he would have lived another ten minutes.

Chapter 21

Irving Shlibovitz and His Orchestra

I helped a friend produce a record for a band from Australia and New Zealand, and we all used to laugh about a real wedding/bar mitzvah band called the Irving Shlibovitz Orchestra. I told the band that the City of Hope once wanted to use the orchestra at a fund-raiser dinner. I had this vision of Mr. Shlibovitz leaning into the microphone and saying, "Now, the accordion player, Nathan, will lead us all in some rock and roll! Hit it, Nate!" Nate would come onstage and belt out, "Tie a yellow ribbon round the old och (eastern European accent simulated) tree."

I vetoed that idea ("Not if you want me there"), and the City of Hope hired a great reggae band instead, although they showed up almost an hour late because the doorman didn't believe a bunch of Rasta-looking guys could be there for one of these fancy charity things. We were all sweating because the doors were set to open—and no band. At 7:20 p.m., ten minutes before start time, they snuck through the kitchen and found me so I could go talk to security and let them in. They weren't wearing their stage clothes yet and looked a little disheveled. My mother walked up and told me, "The next sound you hear will be the sound of your father hitting the floor."

The funny thing was the real Irving Shlibovitz Orchestra was playing for the Fisher wedding next door, had an accordion player named Maury, and was playing "Tie A Yellow Ribbon" as we walked by.

- - - - - - - - - -

The record I helped produce didn't sell. The band dispersed back to their hometowns and took up the rest of their lives. But Irving Shlibovitz and his orchestra were not forgotten.

The singer I worked with came from a small town on the South Island in New Zealand. The local pub was the center of life and the local rugby team the center of everything. He joined a band that played at the pub, and they wrote a song for the rugby team. The rugby team won the New Zealand Premiership, and the song got some national attention in New Zealand.

Later that year, New Zealand hosted the international Rugby World Cup, with an expected television audience over one billion people. The pub got a call asking if the band would play the song at the internationally televised opening ceremonies. They agreed, of course, but then were asked the name of the band, and without thinking the lead singer replied, "The Irving Shlibovitz Orchestra." And there, in front of a hundred thousand screaming fans, every human in New Zealand and a billion people around the world heard the announcer say in that deep stadium voice:

"And now, the Irving Shlibovitz Orchestra..."

Chapter 22

Raoul Wallenberg

For the City of Hope fund-raiser, a friend who was press secretary for a local city councilperson arranged for me to get a proclamation from the City of Los Angeles at the awards dinner. As usual, the city was late in getting the official proclamation done. The press secretary explained to the crowd that what they do in these circumstances is grab any old proclamation lying around the office, flash it for the press (no one ever looks at it or reads it anyway), read what the proclamation is supposed to say, and later send the real one to the recipient.

In my case, he had grabbed one proclaiming Raoul Wallenberg Day. Wallenberg was a Swedish hero, having saved tens of thousands of Jews during WWII, and had been missing for decades. Many thought he was in a Russian jail, so the Raoul Wallenberg Day festivities were designed to put pressure on the Russian government to come clean about Wallenberg.

I knew the press secretary had an artistic and somewhat bent sense of humor. For example, he'd also arranged a proclamation for a bar mitzvah he was throwing for his dog.

As we stood at the podium, he explained all of this to the audience and then said that since I was such a good friend, instead of reading the wording from my proclamation, he would read the proclamation he held and just substitute my name. So he read: "Bob Danziger, the Swedish Angel of Mercy, who saved thousands of Jews during World War Two…"

Part 4

The Road

Oil versus Crocodiles (Juan Ibanez)

Chapter 23

Travels with Sunlaw

Dancing At the Train Station in Tokyo

Being CEO of Sunlaw required that I be a road warrior. I was on a plane going somewhere several times a month. After a trip to Thailand, I headed to Japan for a meeting with Osaka Gas Company, a company with whiskey dispensers on the executive floors and hosts who regularly drank a gallon of beer for lunch. Gene, my operations manager, and I planned to go by train from Tokyo to Osaka. Gene went to get the tickets, and I stood in front of the train station playing my kalimba and guarding the bags. In Thailand, children would gather around or at least notice and smile when I played—it's a very sweet sound—and the same thing happened in Germany, France, Belgium, England, and most other places. At the train station in Tokyo, though, no one so much as looked at me. Some took pains not to look at me.

I figured I was confronting a whole different social norm, but I saw this as a bit of a challenge. I started playing louder. No one listened, no one looked. Still louder. No one. So I start dancing, then doing

Rockette kicks. No one even glanced at me. There I was, some eighteen inches taller than everybody, gravitationally challenged, playing a sweet little African instrument in Tokyo, and dancing. No one looked or listened. I was invisible.

Gay Pride Parade in Boston

I met a colleague in Boston who was planning to visit her boyfriend after our meetings. We met at the airport, and she was wearing a tight red minidress, that fully showed off her chest area ampleness, and a choker. We got in a taxi, but as we neared the hotel, traffic was completely stopped. A parade was going on and the streets were blocked with cheering crowds. The cab driver explained that we could get out and walk the two blocks to the hotel with our luggage or sit there with the meter running and wait for the parade to end and the crowd to disperse.

I took our three bags out of the trunk and we proceeded to the hotel, with Nancy walking ahead of me while I struggled with the suitcases. The sidewalks were thick with people, so we went out partly into the parade street to find a clear path. I heard the old Motown classic "Stop! In the Name of Love" and turned to see a float with several gyrating people all dressed like

Diana Ross and the Supremes on it. Something was off, so I did a double take and realized these were all men dressed like Diana. Right then, two guys pointed at Nancy and said loudly, "Look at the [boobs] on that boy."

To the untrained eye, we were marching in the gay pride parade as part of a cross-dressing group. I remember thinking, *I hope they are not televising this. I don't know how to explain this one to Mom.*

Mr. Chairman

I was flying from Boston to Los Angeles and found myself sitting next to Alan Greenspan, soon to be chairman of the Federal Reserve. I had a keyboard with me and we got to talking about music. He explained that he had worked his way through school playing clarinet and was second chair in a dance band to Stan Getz, who happened to have played at my bar mitzvah. I asked Greenspan if he still played. He said that once a month or so he would pull the clarinet out of the closet to play; it would "feel great in my hands and great in my mouth, but after a while it hurts my ears and I have to stop."

Cab Rides from Hell 1 – Brussels

The convention center in Brussels, Belgium, was about five miles from the hotel I was staying in. I needed to return in the early afternoon and so got in one of the cabs lined up at the convention center. I told the driver to go to the hotel. He slammed the car into gear and stomped the pedal to the floor, and we went skidding and careening into traffic. He started shouting in Flemish at the top of his lungs and took his hands off the wheel, replacing them with his elbows. I was freaking in the back seat, and he was becoming increasingly hysterical, weaving in and out of traffic, keeping the pedal on the floor. Suddenly, he made a fishtailing left turn into what appeared to me to be a one-lane alley, knocking over some trash cans just like in the movies. A small truck was coming right toward us, and we were about to have a head-on collision when the cabbie made another fishtailing right turn into a different alley, still driving with his elbows, still shrieking in Flemish. After a hundred yards, he made a screaming left turn and the cab literally skidded into a parallel park right in front of the hotel. He stopped the car, turned to me, and said, in perfect English, "That will be twelve dollars, and I recommend a two-dollar tip."

About the same as the dry cleaning bill to get the stains out of my pants.

Cab Rides from Hell 2 – Chicago

I get in a cab at my hotel in downtown Chicago. The driver says in a thick Chicago accent, "O'Hare or Midway?" (Chicago's airports). I say I'm going to my cousin's house near Milwaukee and Central Avenues. The cabbie says, "O'Hare or Midway?" I say, "No, not O'Hare or Midway, I'm going to Milwaukee and Central." He shouts, "Milwaukee!" and takes off like a bat out of hell for Milwaukee, Wisconsin, which is about ninety miles away. We're on the freeway to Milwaukee, and I'm in the back hollering at this guy to stop, go back, I'm not going to Wisconsin, and otherwise trying to get this maniac to let me out. Nothing is working. It seems he knows only three words of English: O'Hare, Midway, and Milwaukee.

Finally, I yell, "I'm not paying!" Turns out he knows more English, because he stops right in the middle of the freeway, second lane from the fast lane. It's clear he isn't moving, and cars are whizzing by.

He looks at me and says, in perfect English, just like the cabbie in Brussels, "That will be twenty dollars."

Vattenfall – The Chess Show

Vattenfall is the electric utility for the area around Stockholm and much of the rest of Sweden. I was there on a consulting assignment. It's also where I learned a lot about energy conservation, and particularly about ventilation.

It was my first time in a high-latitude country, so the first night I did the obligatory get up with the sun and go to work—only to find out that it was two in the morning. Since it was summertime, sunrise came early this Sunday.

I couldn't get back to sleep, and around seven or so I went out again to the Kungsflora, a beautiful park in the center of Stockholm that had good street-food vendors and one of those giant chessboards with pieces about three feet tall. Serious banker-looking guys were already having intense matches with much chin rubbing, puffing on pipes, and knowledgeable murmuring from a small crowd gathered in the bleachers adjacent to the board.

I don't play chess, so I don't know, but it was all pretty stately and impressive.

I went back on Wednesday when I had a break from work. The bankers were, of course, at their offices. Instead, the people in the park were the ones you'd expect to be there when people are working—the drunk and homeless.

The quality of the play was a little different, too. They would pass the bottle, accidentally change sides, and then yell at each other for moving the pieces.

Predators' Ball

There was an investment banker in the 1990s who worked in energy finance and threw these incredible spendathon parties for his investors. Later convicted of several felonies and forced to pay a one-billion-dollar fine, Michael Milken was famous for these parties, which were called "Predators' Balls."

Paul was a friend who worked for the same investment house and got me an invite. Paul is of Italian descent and has an eye for the ladies. I decided to invite my neighbor, a model, to be my date for the event. Her mom told me she was concerned about going because all she had were minidresses, which this tall beauty could seriously rock. I assured her mother that a minidress would work just fine.

Milken had rented the Century City Shopping Center and Theatres for the occasion, and everything was free. We ran into Paul and his colleague, and spoke for almost forty-five minutes. The next day he called me, a little angry.

> "How come you didn't come to the party last night? I called in a lot of favors to get you the invite."

> "Paul, I was there, don't you remember?"

> He said no.

> "Paul, do you remember a tall, gorgeous woman in a minidress you talked to for forty-five minutes?"

> "Yes, Bob."

> "Paul, I was the guy standing next to her."

Flying Door in Rochester

My first trip to Rochester, New York, was in the dead of winter, to visit the law firm that had advanced us almost two million dollars in legal services when we had no money. My plane was very late. At two in the morning I finally got a cab to my hotel, a sort of Motel 6.

I like to exercise and needed to work out some kinks from the long day's travel. At the time, I used the rubber exercise bands that you hook into a doorjamb to do a range of exercises. With the anchor in the door, I was lying on the floor in my underwear, sweating and doing overhead pulls, when the frame splintered and the door came off its hinges, then flew over me and right through the window. It was two thirty a.m., I barely had clothes on, and snow was coming in through both the gaping doorway and the broken window.

I never got so cold or dressed so fast in my life. I ran to the front desk, woke up the clerk, and by the time we got back to the room everything was covered with snow.

The Virgin Islands

A big Wall Street investment banking firm engaged Sunlaw to develop a cogeneration project on St. Croix in the U.S. Virgin Islands. The project would have provided electricity and desalinated water to the island and was supposed to replace some worn-out and dirty diesel engines that had limped along for decades.

The utilities were so unreliable that one hotel had cards printed for guests with the motto *"The weather's great, the seas divine, forget the utilities and have a good time."*

The project became quite controversial, especially after the governor fired the entire Water and Power Authority Board of Directors and replaced them with three appointees, two of whom had recently been convicted of crimes but were pardoned by the governor.

This governor was close friends with Mayor Marion Barry of Washington, DC, who was caught on tape smoking crack with a girlfriend.

Not that the governor didn't have a sense of humor. When questioned by a local news crew about how he'd managed to buy a two-and-a-half-million-dollar home on the coast of Spain after never making more than fifteen thousand dollars per year in any job he'd ever held, he looked right in the camera and said:

"The miracle of compound interest."

- - - - - - - - - -

Situations developed and I needed a team of bodyguards. A stunningly beautiful woman, who was also the first female sergeant of a SWAT team in the United States, was the leader.

She had told us the story that, as a rookie, she'd been sent undercover to arrest some male prostitutes. They dressed her up nice, called an escort service, and she got him up to the room fully wired for video and audio, with detectives in the next room.

The suspect looked around and said, "Normally, the women I get called for don't look so good. I'll tell you what, you are so pretty, this one's on the house."

That wasn't part of the plan. The suspect needed to offer sex for money. She didn't know what to do, so she excused herself, went next door to where the detectives were with the audio/video equipment, and asked them what she should do. They exhorted: "Go for it! Go for it!" Sort of an early YouTube thing.

She didn't go for it; she told the guy she was a cop and off he went.

Unfortunately, my bodyguard liked younger men; in fact, she married three nineteen-year-olds in a row before she married someone her own age. I would know when the relationship was coming to an end, because after a year or two I'd get a call from her:

> ***"Bob, I need a conversation."***

- - - - - - - - - -

My regular taxi driver on St. Croix had a PhD in the literature of Shakespeare and a deep voice that complemented the accent of his native Trinidad. He recited Shakespeare in that incredible lilted bass as we drove around the island.

- - - - - - - - - -

The whole situation quickly devolved into litigation after the Water and Power Authority Board repudiated our contract and gave it to a local company called the South Shore group. A few of their members were subsequently indicted by a New Jersey grand jury for involvement with organized crime.

The judge in the case directed us to hold settlement discussions. To keep the discussions private, an elaborate plan was made for participants to meet at the Caribe Hilton in San Juan, Puerto Rico, with some traveling on commercial flights, some on boats, some in private planes, and one in a helicopter. We planned to arrive separately over a three-hour period to avoid being seen together. A suite was reserved, and the appointed day arrived.

Of course, stuff happened and seven of the eight of us arrived at exactly the same time, seven cabs in a row. We were looking at each other, more than a little aghast, when a throng of reporters there to cover George H. W. Bush, the sitting vice president, and Jesse Jackson, then a presidential candidate, crossed directly in front of our startled group. Thousands of pictures were being taken. When we were recognized by a number of regional reporters, our "secret" negotiations were on the air before the meeting even began.

The negotiations didn't pan out, and the trial kicked off a few weeks later. Every facet of the trial was covered by the island's papers. Every witness was a lead story, every rumor all over talk radio. There wasn't much happening in St. Croix, so the juiciness of our courtroom drama made for entertaining reading. For example—and I am not making this up—on the day that I testified, the second lead story was "Dog Bites Boy," and the third-page inside lead was "Waves Still Breaking on the Beach."

One of the first witnesses at the trial was the financial "expert" for a local contractor and disgruntled bidder. When confronted with the fact that his proposal lost money, lots of it, he was asked how he intended to finance this loser. He replied, "RSPs."

Lawyers don't like to ask questions they don't know the answer to, so our lawyer came over and conferred with the investment bankers. They didn't know what an RSP was. I didn't know what an RSP was.

The lawyer hemmed and hawed, then walked back to the witness, and said, "OK, I'll bite; what's an RSP?" With a perfectly straight face, the witness answered, "Rich Stupid People."

It's pretty clear, though, that Rich Stupid People investing with this guy would pretty soon become "PSPs"—Poor Stupid People (Bernie Madoff investors?).

Scrotum in Singapore

The most important conference in the energy world is called Power-Gen, and it is held once in Asia and once in the United States each year. This particular year the Asian conference was in Singapore, and I was going to speak on the results of running the pollution control system on our power plants for thirty thousand hours.

The hotel in Singapore was built over a three-story shopping mall. Near the elevators and escalators was a sort of open shop where massage therapists gave reflexology foot rubs. I sat down and took off my shoes, and this guy started working my feet.

Reflexology is supposed to promote general health, on the theory that each part of the foot is connected to another part of the body. So, if your foot hurts when pressed in a particular spot that indicates the corresponding area in the body needs "healing." The attendant can rub the pain out of the foot, helping the connected organ or whatever.

My therapist found a spot that was tender and told me that it was connected to the lower spine. Then he found another spot near the big toe that was tender, and I asked, "What's that?" He mumbled something.

I asked again, and before he answered, the entire mall became momentarily silent. The escalators stopped, the elevator doors opened, and it seemed that everyone turned to look at us. Then, in a loud voice, loud enough to be heard throughout the mall, he yelled, "Scrotum! It's your scrotum!"

The Czar of Cyanide

I was flying from LA to Baltimore, and my seatmate mentioned that the reason he was flying first class was that Northwest Airlines had given him a free upgrade.

The airline gave him the free upgrade because it had lost his mother's body.

After she died in San Francisco, he'd flown to LA for his mother's burial. Northwest was supposed to fly her body to LA for the ceremony and burial, but had accidentally shipped her to Japan. They loaded her on another plane bound for LA, but during the ten or twelve hours it took for her to get there, all the guests, the minister, and so on had gone home. He was left to bury her, at night, with just a couple of grave diggers.

He could tell I was incredulous, so he took out his ticket; sure enough, right on the bottom was typed:

"Upgrade due to loss of Mother's body."

I asked what he did for a living.

"I'm the czar of cyanide. I used to be the guru of cyanide, but I got a promotion."

"Army weapons lab?" I asked.

"Yes."

Chapter 24

Australia

Beatles, Disney, and the Life Down Under

Sunlaw was generally credited with being the first successful independent energy company in the United States. The Australian government had decided they wanted to increase the sort of alternative energy projects that Sunlaw had been doing, so invited us to bid along with a few other companies on building some new power plants around the country. General Electric sponsored us and paid our way. We eventually ran out of money and had to stop, but it was fun while it lasted.

On that first business trip to Australia, a friend in the music business, Ed Leffler, connected me with Michael Gdinski, head of a big Australian music label, who agreed to show me around town the Friday before I left for the United States.

Ed Leffler was my best friend and golf buddy for many years, and his music industry contacts made my life much more fun. Ed's father was the booking agent for

The Ed Sullivan Show, and his agency would road manage the U.S. tours for bands booked on the show. The Beatles, for example.

Ed actually did the road management for the Beatles in 1964, that first year—and it was his first time on that job. Ed became a big name in the entertainment business and had been offered the CEO position at a number of studios. Instead, he arranged for protégés to get those positions, such as Michael Eisner at Disney.

Disney more or less owned the public utility that serves Disney World in Florida. Mickey Mouse-shaped utility poles were some of the unusual touches. Ed thought Sunlaw could help Disney.

Ed wanted me to meet Eisner. We went to Disney headquarters at the appointed time. Giant pillars shaped like the seven dwarfs framed the entrance to the building. As we went in, Ed told me that he never waited more than twenty minutes for any appointment; we would be gone at twenty minutes, no matter what. I wanted this meeting and prayed Eisner wasn't late. At eighteen minutes, the assistant came to get us.

Ed also knew well the heads of MTV and Paramount and had dated Marilyn Monroe. When he died, his tombstone read: "I didn't miss much." Based on what we knew, his friends felt the tombstone just as easily could have been engraved with: "I didn't miss anything."

- - - - - - - - - -

Michael Gdinski picked me up in his limo and took me to a TV talk show he was appearing on that evening. When we got to the station, he was whisked away by a producer to makeup, and I went into the green room. I'd known Gdinski all of five minutes at this point, but we'd come in the limo together and I was dressed in my all-black suit, so the others in the green room assumed I was close to him.

A handful of people in the room wanted Gdinski to listen to their music and hopefully sign them to his label. Gdinski was known as an admirer of the ladies, so apparently the word was out that if he was approached by a pair (or more) of beautiful, sympathetic, and energetic young ladies, he would listen to the music whilst otherwise engaged. I was in the green room for about ten seconds before these two gorgeous blondes started nuzzling me as one handed me a tape. Pretty soon three brunettes, then two redheads, joined them.

I had no clue what was going on, but I was clearly growing to love Australia fast.

Side You Throw Up Over

Melbourne, Australia, has a state holiday on the day the Melbourne Cup thoroughbred race is held. It's like the Kentucky Derby, except it's held on a weekday and all the schools, businesses, government offices, and so forth are closed for the day.

Australia is a country where:

- When I had a six-hour layover in Cairns, I got in a cab and asked the driver to take me some place tourists don't go, so he took me to his parents' house, where his mom made us raisin bread and I turned wood with his father, a retired policeman.

- When I called the airline to ask if it could help a girlfriend who was afraid of flying, the employees arranged for a group of nuns to pick her up and take her to the airport, and then four of the nuns flew with her to Perth, even though her "confession," had she offered it, would

have taken a lot longer than a six-hour flight—
or two or three—and might have needed a
record number of Hail Marys to rectify.

- Crocodile Dundee Bowie knives were sold in
the lobby of the Parliament building AFTER
you went through security.

- The *Financial Review* (their *Wall Street
Journal*) had a front-page editorial on the
alleged Nancy Reagan-Frank Sinatra affair,
opining:

> It must have been a "very, very dark
> room."

- The American slave-history miniseries *Roots*
was mistakenly thought to be a comedy
because "rooting" is an Australian slang word
for having sex; after the broadcast, a review the
next day read: "Not very funny."

- A friend's sixteen-year-old daughter was
working in a convenience store, and when a
young man she had a crush on came in, she
laughed so hard her dress came off. They've
been together ever since. Seems like a good

evolution of the species to me—if she fancies you, her dress just falls off.

- In Melbourne, a local attorney told us about his recent trip to London. The fellow sitting next to him died just before the meal service. The flight attendant explained to the attorney that because of the length of the flight there was a second crew on board, and they were sleeping in the crew seats where normally a dead passenger would be placed. She asked if the dead person could be left strapped in the seat beside him, and then said,

> "But don't worry, you can have his dessert."

He took two free first-class tickets instead.

So maybe it's not so strange that they would have a state holiday for a horse race in the middle of the week. And I was there, invited by a client, looking for a hat. No hats for sale. No hats. Turns out the Melbourne Cup features elaborate headwear—Easter bonnet sort of stuff, with all kinds of decorations and historical scenes playing out about the follicles. But it was a sunny day and no hats were for sale. I was very white and burning very red.

I heard a lady I'd never met before say, "John, give him your hat." He answered, "I don't want to give him my hat; it's my favorite hat." She looked at me, pointed, and told him, "He's burning up; give him your hat." I was more than a little surprised, having never met these folks in my life, but he walked over and gave me his hat. I promised to return the hat, take them to dinner, and play a song for them. They gave me their phone numbers and such, but Rasa, the wife, said they were inviting me to their home for dinner, and I certainly didn't need to take them out.

I went over on the appointed evening and noticed Olympic medals, large replicas of great America's Cup yachts, and other sailing and sport memorabilia. It turned out that the guy who had given me his hat was John Bertrand, the first person to win the America's Cup away from the United States in its 132-year history. At the time, John was the most famous person in Australia, beating out all the founders, politicians, actors, and inventors.

Australians love their sport—they once interrupted a telecast of a speech by the prime minister to report an

Australian's progress in a lawn bowling tournament in England.

Also at the dinner were Ron and Cheryl Barassi, and he was the second most famous man in Australia because of his accomplishments in Australian Rules Football as player, coach, and national commentator.

I commuted to Australia for my job, and the Bertrands and Barassis sort of adopted me when I was Down Under. We got to know each other pretty well. John was making another run at the America's Cup, to be held about three years later in San Diego. He asked me to attend a meeting in Sydney that was to be the kickoff for the challenge. I had never been on a sailboat or to a race, so I asked why, and he told me he wanted someone with no preconceptions to challenge everything, and he thought I could be a good "lateral thinker." So I went.

The kickoff meeting was held in an office with a beautiful view of Sydney Harbor. Sitting next to me was Lindsay Cunningham, who had many times won the Little America's Cup, which is a solo catamaran race, and he was very respected by John and the other professional sailors in the room.

The talks started and the speakers all used lots of nautical terms and acronyms, so I had no clue what they were talking about. They had a shorthand that was a new language to me. When a term came up, I'd lean over to Lindsay and ask, "What's that?" and he'd explain. "MWSA" (Maximum Wetted Surface Area) and "VPP" (Velocity Prediction Program) were explained under his breath as the talks went on.

The terms "windward" and "leeward" came up fairly frequently, and I leaned over to Lindsay and asked what these were. He couldn't believe anybody could be in a meeting about this level of sailing and not know such basic terms, and figured I had been jerking him around on all the other questions. He refused to answer any more questions and glared at me.

At the break, I cornered him and explained that I really didn't know, I really was that ignorant, and could he please explain what "leeward" and "windward" meant. He started talking about convex versus concave, the luff of the sails, and so on. He must have seen my confusion deepening because he stopped his explanation, looked at me, and said,

"Leeward is the side you throw up over."

- - - - - - - - - -

I also composed and recorded the music played for the team as it pulled out of the harbor. The New Zealanders had this strong Maori chant and warrior dance they did, and it was intimidating. *OneAustralia* wanted something from their aboriginal heritage to counteract the Maori magic.

Yothu Yindi was a popular aboriginal music group that had crossed over into mainstream pop by remixing some traditional music with a disco/hip-hop kind of beat. There was one particular "didgeridoo" piece that John and the crew liked, and they asked me to see if I could license it. I was put in contact with the group and learned that the correct aboriginal term for didgeridoo is "yidaki." Yothu Yindi had serious reservations about helping a sports effort sponsored by a beer company because alcoholism was a problem they were fighting in their community. Besides, they noted that they had not written the song. Some other people they knew had written it, and they'd have to ask for permission to license it to us.

About two weeks later I asked the band members if they had an answer. They explained that they had gone into "dreamtime" to contact the composers, their ancestors who had lived forty thousand years ago. For aboriginals of this area, dreams are considered real, and what we think of as awake, they consider like a dream. They told me that they had a long discussion with the ancient composers.

I asked what their ancestors had decided about licensing the song to us.

"They said no."

- - - - - - - - - -

The *OneAustralia* team had the distinction of being the first in the history of this famous sailing competition to have one of its boats sink.

OneAustralia was sailing against its archrivals, the New Zealanders, when the boat sank. *OneAustralia* had pushed a little too hard, and the sea and wind split the boat right in half. The team had been sponsored by Foster's beer, so there was a giant Foster's beer can on the ship's sail, which was videotaped sinking rapidly beneath the waves. Steinlager (another beer company), sponsored the Kiwis. The company purchased large blocks of national advertising in Australia for that night and showed a commercial with the Australian boat sinking, followed by an image of the Steinlager logo, while the announcer said:

> *"Steinlager, the only thing that goes down faster than a Foster's."*

The Barassis

From that dinner at the Bertrands', a lifelong friendship with Cheryl and Ron Barassi developed. Cheryl, in particular, has been a friend and confidante, and source of some of the deepest laughs I've ever had. The Barassis are funny, irreverent, accomplished, brave, and a lot of other things.

- - - - - - - - - -

Cheryl told me that once they were having the "How come I always have to pick up and clean up after you" argument, and Ron looked down at her and said, "Because I can hold out longer than you."

Cheryl had been to Cairns in northeast Australia and told me that a fellow next to her at a restaurant was having a steak, and she, a vegetarian, had bitingly asked him if he knew how the animal had been raised and how it had died. The steak eater replied that yes, he did know how it died: "You [the vegetarian] ate all of its food."

- - - - - - - - - -

A year or so ago Ron saved a woman being beaten by a gang, so they beat him up instead. A real-life hero, and all of it caught on videotape. Their fame took off like a rocket. A BBC reporter asked Cheryl if she had any advice for Australian men. I can't tell you what she replied—very X-rated and very funny—but if you see me, make sure to ask me to tell you the rest of this story.

How Did She Knock on the Door?

Georgia was a woman who made other women's heads swivel. A choreographer for music videos, she knew sexy and she knew how to move. She had become a very good friend, nothing more, because she was a lesbian.

I loved going out with her, though, because I'm schlumpy and not one of the beautiful people, and because when someone, often a beautiful girl, often right in front of me, would ask her why she was with me, Georgia would look her right in the eye and tell her it was because I gave the best sex in the western hemisphere. She had no way of knowing she was right, of course, but we both loved watching these people slink away.

Then one day, I was in my usual room at the Park Hyatt in Sydney overlooking the opera house, ferry terminal, and the bridge, when I heard a loud knock on my door. I opened the door and saw Georgia standing there in wicked heels, fishnets, a baby-doll negligee, and a choker. The next thing I noticed was that her hands were cuffed behind her back. I remember thinking,

How did she knock on the door?

- - - - - - - - - -

Right then, a group of Japanese businessmen came through on a tour conducted by the hotel manager, a tall, stately blonde in her fifties. She stopped, looked at me and at Georgia, gave me a big smile, and walked on, with the businessmen bumping into each other as they tried not to look.

- - - - - - - - - -

The Hyatt manager and I also became friends, and she had special robes made for me and Luciano Pavarotti because we were the same size and the standard hotel robes fit neither of us. Pavarotti stayed one floor above me when he was in Sydney to perform at the opera house; he, in room 314, and I in room 214.

The Chinese restaurant next door also got into the act. They had one of those giant black lacquer Chinese imperial-type chairs they kept in a hallway on the ground floor. Whenever one of us walked by, the owner would chase us down the promenade holding the chair over his head, shouting, "You and Pavarotti, you and Pavarotti, only ones allowed to sit in this chair!" The only way to shut him up was to slow down so he could catch up and then sit in the chair for a moment or two. Good food with a side of public humiliation.

Shelf Reef and Soprano Giants

One of the nice things about flying back and forth to Australia was that you could stop at South Seas islands, such as Tahiti and Fiji, as well as the Great Barrier Reef at no extra charge. One special spot is on the island of Savusavu in Fiji, where the pilots circle the field to chase off the cows before they land. That's where I learned to scuba dive, and the underwater world opened up to me.

At the dock one day, some fellows from California talked to a captain about chartering his boat to do some fishing. The captain and other Fijians at the dock gave each other glances, then started laughing after the fishermen went back to their hotel. I asked the captain why they were laughing.

He said he'd show me, and drove me in his beat-up old truck to a beach on the opposite side of the island. "A shelf reef," he said. And while we sat there for an hour or so, the ocean moved to low tide, and sure enough, a large reef, stretching maybe a mile into the ocean, rose from the lowering water. Geysers spouted ten to fifteen feet into the air as waves pushed water through unseen crevices to explode in curtains as fancy as the great fountains of Europe, only wild and changing. We got out of the truck and walked out on the reef, avoiding the geysers, and he pointed to fish as big as a large tuna and hundreds of other smaller fish that were stranded on the reef.

When locals wanted fish, they waited for low tide and then just went out to the reef and picked them up. Rods, reels, hooks, and bait were unnecessary, let alone chartering a boat to fish! Why would anyone want to do that?

At the village every night at sunset, everyone would come out to watch the light show, drink kava, and sing. A beautiful tradition they believe is forty thousand years old—the same age as Yothu Yindi's ancestors. The funny part, though, was that the bigger the man, the higher he was expected to sing. It was kind of a virility thing for them. So these giant guys would be singing soprano to a setting sun in one of the most beautiful and friendliest places on earth. I couldn't sing that high with a ladder.

Chapter 25

The Presidents

Irish in Australia – Jew from LA

When in Melbourne, I usually stayed at the Hyatt, and after I did that once or twice a month for a year or so, the staff started giving me the same room. It was a regular room on the top floor, next to the fire escape and across the hall from the presidential suite. I had never seen any presidents in it, but occasionally the staff would let me in to play the grand piano or use the twelve-person Jacuzzi.

Returning to the hotel after work one day, I saw that they were moving all the guests from the top floor to lower floors, and two or three security people now sat in each of the rooms, but with the doors open. They weren't the hotel security. They were the security detail for the president of Ireland, who, I learned, was staying in the presidential suite for the next few days. They all wore green ties.

I asked one of the hotel people what room I was being moved to, and she told me that I was well-known and could stay in my room. I was the only civilian left on the whole floor. They had obviously gone out of their way to keep me on the floor and were pleased with themselves. Without going into detail, let's just say that running a gauntlet of security people every day was going to cramp my style a little.

The next morning I felt a little rumble, and it turned out the IRA had detonated a small explosive near the valet parking that tore a fair-sized chunk out of the street. I didn't know the IRA was mad at the president of Ireland as well as half of Northern Ireland, but apparently she was worth a small explosive to them.

As I left my room, I noticed large portraits of early Irish settlers in Melbourne in elaborate frames stacked against the back door to the presidential suite.

This bit of geography is important. Next to my door was the fire escape door, and next to the fire escape, across the hall, was the back door to the presidential suite, set in a sort of shallow alcove. The front door to the presidential suite was fifty feet or so away from the fire escape and in the direction of the elevators. The large portraits were against the back door across the hallway from my room.

Returning to the hotel in the early evening, I strolled off the elevator into a crush of security people, military officers, local police, and hotel staff. Around 150 fretting people were crowded into the area between the elevators and my room, and I wound my way through the unsettled throng. I got to my door and noticed that the Irish settler paintings were still leaning against the president's back door.

I dropped off my briefcase in my room and went back to find out what was up. I asked one of the Irish security people, with whom I had a nodding acquaintance, about the pictures, and he shot back, "What pictures?" I told him about the big pictures in the shallow alcove by the back door. He shouted at the top of his lungs:

"Pictures around the corner!"

Then he ran the fifty feet to the end of the hall, followed by maybe a hundred of the 150 people who had been standing around. In the small space, they were comically piling on and bouncing off each other when a woman in a naval-looking uniform materialized and started furiously pumping my hand, saying:

"You've done a great service to Ireland; you've done a great service to the Republic."

I had no clue what was going on, and right then, the door to the presidential suite opened and Mary Robinson, the president of Ireland, was there. The bumping and bouncing stopped, and the naval-looking person announced to the president:

"Give this man a medal. This man deserves a medal; he found the pictures."

The president said, "Great," and the officer proclaimed that I would be made an honorary citizen of Ireland. The president closed the door, the officer took my card to do the honorary citizen thing, and people lined up to shake my hand. (Note: I regrettably never heard from her. I'd love to be an honorary Irish citizen—I love that music.)

I still had no clue and was looking around for somebody to tell me what the hell was going on. Finally, someone explained that the pictures were an official gift from Australia to Ireland, and were supposed to have been delivered to the presidential suite. When the paintings weren't found in the suite, military reserves had been brought in to search every room, nook, and cranny of the thirty-two-story hotel. That's what all those people were there for—they'd spent the entire day searching for these missing national treasures.

But nobody, apparently, walked the fifty feet to the end of the hall and checked either the fire escape or the BACK DOOR of the presidential suite.

After I went to my room, it dawned on me: bombs, directed at this president who was staying across the hall, had gone off that morning and no one had walked down the hall or checked the fire escape. Increasingly nervous, I left my room to ask the Irish security guy if he could make sure to check the whole hallway, and especially the fire escape. He brushed me off, saying it was taken care of, no big deal, don't worry, we have it under control. I got persistent. I said that really, with bombs going off, could he promise to wander near my door from time to time. He wouldn't commit.

I went back to my room and made a large sign that read:

"Dear Terrorist, I am a Jew from the United States. Door to the presidential suite is down the hall on the left."

I left the room to ask the security guy for tape so I could put it on my door. The security guy read the sign, sighed, and said, "OK, we'll check. We promise, we'll check."

President of Mexico

In a bizarre twist, my next set of meetings was in southern Mexico, so I decided to rest a couple of days in Cancun after meetings in Campeche. My plane from Mérida arrived late, so I didn't get to the hotel until around one a.m. I took off my clothes and had a nice soak in the Jacuzzi on the balcony under the stars. The next morning I woke up around ten and went out in my birthday suit for another dip in the Jacuzzi on what I assumed was a private balcony.

It turned out the balcony wasn't private at all, and the president of Mexico had moved into the room next to mine sometime between two and ten that morning. Hundreds of machine-gun-armed guards were all over the place, and in particular on all the balconies adjacent to my very non-private one. Two ships were anchored offshore with their guns pointed to either side of the president's room; i.e., there were large cannons pointed at my pop gun.

I was surprised, and suddenly very awake. I backed slowly into my room, even though the soldiers could easily see that I was, shall we say, poorly armed.

Part 5

Music Man

Chapter 26

Bob the Musician

You've probably figured out that music is a big part of my life. I tried being a full-time professional, but that didn't work out. I was lucky, though, because I was able to make music a fun and balancing part of my life and the source of many great stories.

I was a normal teenage boy—modestly antisocial behavior masked a lot of much deeper antisocial behavior. But I was fortunate to have skilled adult role models to hone my bad habits and pleasurable irresponsibility—musicians.

I had played a little piano, cello, and trumpet as I grew up, none well. In one of those weird twists of fate, working as a roofer I broke my back when a ladder broke. I had just turned eighteen, and I spent the next ten months lying flat on my back in bed, constantly playing a bass guitar. Musicians call this "woodshedding," and I got out of bed in love with R & B, blues, and the bass guitar, determined to become a studio and concert musician.

Is the Music Backward?

Cecil Taylor has been a controversial avant-garde jazz figure for over thirty-five years, composing and playing what some would describe as atonal music using very complex rhythms. Not accessible to all, it is still loved by some. I had never heard anything about it until one summer day in Yellow Springs, Ohio.

I had just started attending Antioch College, a now-defunct university well versed in protest and counterculture. I was allowed to lock up my bass amplifier in the auditorium storage area, and I'd go there to practice when the auditorium was empty.

I'd taken up the bass guitar only about a year before, although I'd played some stand-up bass since the sixth grade. My cousin Maury owned a music shop, and brought me a hollow body bass guitar to play after I'd broken my back working as a roofer. I learned to play it lying down, and also learned to make all kinds of sound effects like thunder, talking sounds, scratching, popping, and so on. I had a lot of time on my hands, along with the energy of an eighteen-year-old, and I was in bed twenty-two hours a day for ten months, so I played that bass guitar almost every minute. I could make sounds on the electric bass no one had heard before.

So there I was in the Antioch auditorium, making these weird sounds mixed with R & B, funk, and blues. A short, intense man wearing a wool bucket hat came down the aisle, stopped, and listened. When I paused, he asked if I'd like to try out for the band. I said sure and he told me to come back at eight. I asked who he was and he said Cecil Taylor.

I went over to the campus radio station and asked for some of Cecil's music to listen to before the audition. I was handed a reel-to-reel tape. I threaded the tape machine, started the tape, and this wall of sound emerged. I thought the tape was in backward. I really did. I'd certainly never heard any music like that before.

The DJ who was helping convinced me the tape was in properly and that I was listening to Cecil's music. For some reason it felt pretty good to me (and it turned out that I had some generational connection to his story).

I showed up at eight. No one was there. I had forgotten that eight o'clock is not the same for musicians. So I had an hour or so to myself to set up, warm up before some other musicians came in, and then a little later Cecil walked up and handed me some sheets of paper with numbers and lines and letters and odd references to states of matter. I recognized this as some form of music notation, although I had no clue what it was directing me to do.

So everybody was milling around, and I started playing my weird sounds, looking at the papers but not really thinking about them. I was just having fun to warm up and work out the kinks before the audition started. After a while I stopped, looked up, and noticed that it was quiet and everyone was looking at me. Cecil said, "That was perfect."

And I was in the band. We rehearsed seventy hours a week for three straight months, and that was the end of my undergraduate education and the beginning of my life education.

Bob the Studio Musician

I returned from the Cecil Taylor experience to the family home in Los Angeles, ready to start pursuing the studio musician dream. Never did make much money, but had some great experiences:

- A producer called me to do gravel-type vocals on a record for an artist, Squeaky, a transvestite who billed herself as the first all-girl one-man band.

- At one of my first paid recording sessions with some of Motown's studio folks, we'd warmed up and the producer counted down to start the song. There was no music, no discussion, no nothing. I stood there confused, not playing, and the producer stopped everybody and said, "Big Bob, what's the problem?" I asked what the song was about, what key it was in, chords, something. The producer replied, "Here at Motown we use the FWI system. You *fuck-with-it* until we hear something we like."

- Mongo Santamaria was one of my heroes of Latin jazz, and his manager called me to substitute one night for the bass player, who was sick. The bass player had come to the music shop where I worked, so I guess he made the recommendation. I was pretty nervous when I arrived for the gig, and the manager handed me this stack of "charts," i.e., music, that was the most complex I'd ever seen. It looked like a kid had poured black ink on the page. I played music by ear—I didn't read music very well and had no idea of even where to begin. I must have had a stricken look on my face because the manager said, "We'll get someone else for the second set. Play softly."

• One time a famous singer owed me two hundred fifty dollars for some sessions I'd done for him. Rent was due and I needed the money. I'm not into cocaine, but Steve was a notorious addict, spending more on cocaine in a week than I made in an entire year. His dealer was a guy who called himself Dracula, had two bodyguards, always wore a full-length mink coat, and traveled in a souped-up Mustang. One bodyguard stayed by the car and the other accompanied Dracula to the studio. I hit up Steve's music director for some of the cash owed me. Steve came over and, in front of Dracula, handed me a bag with white powder in it and said, "Here, take this. It's worth more than two hundred and fifty dollars." This did me no good. I needed cash to pay the landlord and would have had to sell the cocaine to pay the rent. I looked at Steve and said, "I've got to pay the rent, and you want me to go into competition with him"—pointing at Dracula—"to do it?" Dracula, who was six foot six, looked down at me and drawled, "Smart boy."

• I went to New York to make my fortune as a studio musician like my cousin, Maury Stein. Maury's brother, Jule Styne, was a big-time Broadway producer and songwriter. I asked Maury for Jule's phone number, thinking he could get me a job in an orchestra or something. Maury told me it wouldn't do any good, but he would give me the number because I had to hear what the receptionist said. I got to New York, called the office, explained who I was, and the person responded, "I'm sorry, Mr. Styne has a policy of NEVER returning phone calls to anyone who claims to be a relative. Thank you very much." Click.

When I got to New York, in a borrowed car with all my worldly possessions, in the first ten minutes I got forced onto a sidewalk by a bus driving on the wrong side of the street, got out of the car and saw a drunk pointing at a fire hydrant and laughing, and saw another drunk walking a chair down the street on a heavy leash with a spiked collar who turned to yell at the chair every few seconds for not keeping up.

Welcome to the Big Apple! Here's your free serving of crazy!

Maury Stein

My cousin Maury. This man deserves his own book.

I was nineteen and worked in Maury's musical instrument shop across the street from the Musicians' Union Local 47 in Hollywood. I sold guitars and tried to appear worldly.

Maury was an A-list studio musician. He was truly beloved by men who were great musicians, drinkers, druggies, porno addicts, and players of all kinds. Five of his mistresses were at his funeral. Two went to his and his wife's fiftieth wedding anniversary. He was the perfect role model for an adolescent heterosexual, and not a bad one for all the other kinds of (fill-in-the-blank) sexuals.

Some examples:

- For decades Maury and the guys from Musicians' Union Local 47 played a gig at a nudist colony, and every year took a group photo dressed in ties, fedoras, and silly grins, holding their instruments.

- The every-night party after work at Maury's musical instrument store ended with Maury playing "Turkey in the Straw" on a Stradivarius and both of his parakeets dancing on the end of his Hill bow as he played.

- For decades the local porn salesman showed up every Wednesday at ten a.m. (the crack of dawn by musician standards), showed a couple of films, and then sold his inventory. I swear the guy looked like a beaver.

The Last Maury Story

Maury had heart attacks fairly often—he had five of them between the ages of fifty-five and seventy-five, when he officially died. I think he was in his early sixties when he died, but he didn't lie down until his mid-seventies.

When Maury went to the cardiac care unit at Cedars-Sinai Hospital near Beverly Hills, notices were posted at the Musicians' Union, word got around, and within twenty-four hours the unit was filled with musicians. Drinks were being mixed in the bedpans while vodka bottles hung from the IV. A pungent smoky odor spilled out of the unit's door. Pills and powders lay on the pizza boxes, which I'm pretty sure didn't come from the pharmacy or the nutritionist. The uniforms of the young, pretty nurses were askew, and they had faraway looks on their smiling faces. I even saw two patients dancing in their beds to "Bill Bailey" in a coordinated routine they'd worked on in recovery after heart bypass surgery. Into all this—and I swear this is true— walked one of the great saxophone players of all time, Stan Getz, who got off the freight elevator naked except for a patient smock and his tenor sax and marched into the unit playing "When the Saints Come Marching In."

It worked to heal Maury every time except the last one.

- - - - - - - - - -

At Maury's funeral, Jule Styne and Maury's wife sat together in the front row. My family sat behind them. Musicians filled all the other seats except the second row across the aisle, where Maury's five mistresses sat together. The rabbi and Maury had never met, so when he got to the standard part of the service about "And he was a good and faithful husband," all in attendance—and I am not making this up—put their faces in their armpits and chortled.

Chapter 27

Kings of the Beach

Two close friends were in the fitness business, one a writer and the other a trainer. The trainer married another trainer, and a few years later they had a baby. You know how parents often project their own fantasies and goals onto their children? My sister called me up when her son was born and said, "He looks like a doctor!" Trust me, he's a great kid, but he doesn't look like a doctor. When my trainer friends had their baby boy, Douglas called me up and said, "You should see the pecs on this kid!"

Trust me, no pecs.

Anyway, the writer, trainer, and I had this little informal pact that when one of us published something we'd sneak in a mention of the others somewhere. If I was working on a song, I might credit Neil and Douglas in the trumpet section or put them in the acknowledgments, something small. Douglas wrote a number of books on training, and often used me as a subject (fortunately not the "before" picture) and put Neil in the acknowledgments.

Neil was engaged to write a book on beach volleyball. Sinjin Smith and Karch Kiraly were the big names at that time and were featured in the book. In the introduction, Neil listed many of the great "Kings of the Beach" from the years before Sinjin, the early years, you might say. And for fun, he slipped my name right in the middle of them.

Without elaborating, since you don't know me, let's just say that most of the body fat in this group is concentrated in me, and to the untrained eye the difference between me jumping and me standing is hard to distinguish. I'm a little light on liftoff. OK, I'm an overweight guy who can't jump; no one mistakes me for a "King of the Beach."

A couple years after the book was published, while at some restaurant in San Diego I ran into a maître d' whose name I recognized as being that of one of the famous volleyball players of old. I told him the story, and he told me that every few weeks all the players had dinner together, and almost every time they'd ask, "Who the f— is Bob Danziger?"

Conclusion

Final Word

I had a lot of fun writing this book. It started when I was writing an article on acid mine drainage and after an hour or two was thoroughly depressed. Concentrating on the funny was a much-needed escape that suddenly took on a life of its own.

A friend suggested that my "narrative involves the initial dream" of actually achieving energy independence, a clean environment, and prosperity. Ups and downs were followed by historic, sometimes off-the-wall, successes. And some bad things happened that tarnished the dream a bit, and made me, in his words, "sadder but wiser." I'm not much of a sad person, though, so maybe "older but wiser" fits a little better.

In the 1980s a report came out that grabbed media attention: a thirty-five-year-old single woman had a better chance of being killed by a terrorist than finding a successful marriage. I was watching CNN and the news reader was an attractive woman in her late thirties. She read a series of stories: hurricane kills twelve; economy tanking, suicides up; child abuse; father kills family. Each story was delivered professionally and calmly.

She read the story about a woman her age having a better chance of being killed by a terrorist, slumped in her seat, and moaned, "Now that's depressing."

This story makes the point that in a world of natural and man-made disasters happening every day, personal life still dominated the emotional landscape of this news anchor's life. As family and loved ones dominate almost everyone's life. It's what binds us all across borders, generations, and ideologies.

A woman at the gym where I work out was complaining about her boyfriend.

> "He never opens up to me about his work. He never tells me about his day. He's distant and cold, especially when I try to get him to open up about his job."

> "What does he do?" I asked.

"He's the technology director for the Central Intelligence Agency."

Maybe my expectations, like hers, were a little unrealistic.

Linus Pauling Groupie

Linus Pauling is one of my heroes. The first man to win two Nobel Prizes, the first for chemistry and the second for peace. I know this because I was flipping through the channels one day when I heard an interviewer ask an elderly gentleman, "How did you get so many great ideas to win two Nobel Prizes?" He replied, "We're not on this earth to have great ideas; we're on this earth to have ideas and a principle of selection."

The statement was riveting, like being struck by a bolt of lightning, and by lightning, I mean genius. I stared at the TV. Who was this guy? It was Linus Pauling. Dr. Linus Pauling.

What I didn't know, but learned many years later, after having heard Linus introduced as "the first man to win two Nobel Prizes" countless times, was that he was actually the second person to win twice. A woman, Marie Curie, won the Nobel Prize for physics in 1903 and for chemistry in 1911. First man, but second person.

I met Dr. Pauling on a flight from San Jose. The seat next to mine was the only one still empty, and I heard a voice say, "Is that seat empty?" I looked up and it was Linus Pauling, and for probably the only time in my life I gushed like a groupie and literally shouted, "Linus Pauling!" Embarrassed, he quickly sat down beside me, then people came up to him for his autograph or just to say hello.

I had a chance to ask him if the quote above was accurate, and he said, "Sounds like something I might have said."

- - - - - - - - - -

Dr. Gene Guth was my chief chemist at Sunlaw. His son, Dr. Ted, handled environmental matters for Sunlaw and arranged for us to hire Gene after he retired as chief chemist at TRW, where he co-invented rocket fuels and the air bag. Gene knew Linus Pauling and arranged for us to discuss the greenhouse gas CO_2. I was interested in designing an atom or molecule that would want to combine with CO_2 and loosen CO_2's bonds so we could make it into something useful instead of a threat. We'd planted a hundred thousand trees, studied throwing CO_2 into the sea or underground, and were supporting wind and solar energy. We knew that separating CO_2 would be easier to do in a natural gas power plant than a coal-fired one.

Natural gas-fired power plants put out a lot less greenhouse gases than power plants that use coal or oil, but they still put out a lot. We'd made a profit in eliminating three other pollutants, so maybe we could do the same for CO_2.

We started working on it. Linus Pauling had started speculating on a geometry for an atom or molecule that could do the job, but unfortunately Dr. Pauling died before we could complete the work.

I know this is supposed to be a funny book, but if someone out there knows someone interested in theoretical chemistry, this is an area I think deserves further study. If you are a theoretical chemist, what are you reading silly books like this one for? GET BACK TO WORK.

But seriously, to all those folks out there in the trenches, working every day for energy independence and a clean environment coupled with prosperity, despite seemingly insurmountable obstacles, I love you and thank you. Now,

GET BACK TO WORK.

Appendix I:

What I Do

Consultant, lawyer, inventor, and/or member of advisory board. Examples are Khosla Ventures (biotech due diligence); National Semiconductor (smart grid), Goal Line Environmental technology (catalysis, nanotechnology), Calera (cement from seawater and CO_2), Gridpoint (smart grid, electric and hybrid vehicles); Google (electric and hybrid vehicles), Carmel Highlands Inventions (electricity from the non-carbon portions of coal, acid mine drainage remediation, in-situ coal gasification), and Cogentrix (CO_2 management options for coal-fired power plants focusing on making wood or masonry-substitute materials from greenhouse gasses).

Lecturing. I currently lecture on a range of energy and environmental areas, and recently lectured at Stanford University and Jet Propulsion Laboratory on "The Emerging Framework for New Energy and Environmental Technologies," which examines the practical requirements to achieve an 80 percent reduction in greenhouse gas emissions by 2050. Of particular note is a January 2005 lecture in which I publicly predicted that oil prices would fall below thirty-five dollars a barrel within three to five years. Other lectures have covered grid-interactive vehicles, biofuels, potential climate change solutions, and ocean issues.

Invention: I am co-inventor on three pending patents. One is for making electricity from the non-carbon parts of coal, and the other two are for a method of making cement from the greenhouse gases and other pollutants from power plants. In addition, I have five issued patents: two on catalyst chemistry for ultra-low emissions from gas-fired power plants, and two on mechanical systems for pollution control. The fifth issued patent is for "The Walking Chair," a medical assistive device I invented to help with my back problems. I also have been involved with hundreds of research and development activities, many of which led to inventions by others.

Music: Five albums (*Never Dreamed, Best of Bob Danziger, One Rock, 1910 Nocturne*, and *Unspoken Dreams*) on iTunes, CD Baby, and other fine download sites. The sound sculpture *Steinbeck's Chinatown* was composed as part of an exhibition by the National Steinbeck Center in Salinas, California. The sound sculpture *1910 Nocturne* played as part of the exhibition Painting by Moonlight at the Monterey

Museum of Art (April 2009 to December 2009). Acoustic percussion on *Some Things Never Change* by Supertramp (1999) and *Meteor* by The Shazam (August 2009). The Supertramp album achieved platinum sales in Germany and France.

Honors and Awards:

- Established Environmental Protection Agency (EPA) Lowest Achievable Emissions Rate (LAER) designation for NOx, CO, and ammonia, and established new Best Available Control Technology (BACT) standard
- Set several world records for safety, reliability, capacity factor, and emissions reductions
- Designated a "Pioneer Qualifying Facility" by the California Public Utilities Commission
- Clean Air Award, South Coast Air Quality Management District (1998)
- City of Los Angeles Commendation by the City Council (council members from the 6th, 10th, and 11th districts) "for good citizenship, social conscience and many contributions to making people breathe easier through the development of forward-looking innovative pollution-control equipment for industrial applications" (June 7, 1996)

- ASCAP Special Award for Adult Alternative, Jazz, World, Special Event, Movie, or Television (July 1996)

Education:

Whittier Law School
JD, Alternative Energy Law, 1975–1978, Law Review

Private Tutors
Chemistry, chemical engineering, mechanical engineering, physics, 1975–1977

Committee of Bar Examiners
College equivalency exam, 1975

Appendix II:

A Little More About My Power Plants

Several people asked for a brief appendix that tells a bit more about my power plants.

My power plants were called "cogeneration" because they produced both electricity for sale to Southern California Edison, and refrigeration for two of the largest cold storage warehouses. Blatant plug: Angelo Antoci and Sam Perricone, with U.S. Growers Cold Storage, are two of my closest friends. Use them. They are the best. Federal Cold Storage was sold to a conglomerate—not the same thing. When Sunlaw started, these two companies supplied over half the cold storage for the Los Angeles area, to give you an idea how much refrigeration my two plants provided.

That's a lot of ice cream sandwiches. In addition the plants produced around sixty megawatts—enough electricity for about sixty thousand homes. The plants ran twenty-four hours a day, seven days a week, for almost fifteen years, with two weeks of maintenance shutdown per year.

We produced the electricity by burning natural gas, although we could burn diesel in an emergency but never had to. Shows you how reliable our natural gas pipeline delivery system is. When you think about it, it's an amazing engineering achievement. The electric grid is also an amazing engineering feat, but it's in your face all the time in the form of utility poles and wires cluttering up the view. The natural gas system is out of sight.

We burned the gas in jet engines made by General Electric that were adapted to make electricity instead of fly a plane. We used the same engine as those used on Boeing 747s and other jumbo jets.

Not everyone knows that the air that comes in the front of a jet engine gets shot out the back of the engine really fast. Even fewer people know that the air coming out of the engine is really hot—about twice as hot as your home oven on broil, and the air that comes out of a car engine.

This hot air has a lot of energy in it. At Sunlaw's power plants the heat was directed into a giant version of the radiator on your car. This is called a heat recovery steam generator, because unlike your car, which needs the coolant to stay liquid, our plants made as much steam as possible.

The steam went several places, but mostly it was used to make more electricity, and some went to making refrigeration for the cold storage warehouses.

The electricity is made in a steam turbine generator. Basically it's the same steam generator that has been in use for over one hundred years. The only difference is that the source of the steam is the waste heat from the jet engine.

The refrigeration also was made from the steam, from the waste heat of the jet engine. Called absorption refrigeration, it is unlike the mechanical refrigeration process used by the refrigerator in your house, which uses a compressor. It's more or less the same kind of refrigerator used in motor homes that run on propane, except our refrigerator was four stories tall.

Limited partners included Prince and two of the Jackson Five brothers with whom I went to Fairfax High School. The power plants were shut down and sold around 2002.

Quotes and Compliments

Breathing Out
Robert A. Jones, Column in the Los Angeles Times, Wednesday, February 5, 1997

Sometimes it's the little stories that are most fun. They can tell us more about ourselves, and how we operate as a culture, than the big stories. This little story begins down in Vernon, the belly of the industrial beast in L.A. If it's big and ugly, it probably gets made in Vernon. As the saying goes, Vernon may not be hell; it just smells like it.

Smack in the middle of Vernon sits a little company known as Sunlaw Energy Corp. In 1995, Sunlaw did a remarkable thing. It built a new generating plant for electricity at the corner of Downey and Fruitland.

Nothing so remarkable about that except this plant probably spews fewer pollutants than any other fossil-fuel plant in the world. In fact, "spews" is the wrong word to use with the Sunlaw plant. On a moderately smoggy day in L.A., the emissions coming out of its stack are cleaner than the air surrounding it.

Or to put it another way, the plant is five times cleaner than required by the South Coast Air Quality Management District. It's more than twice as clean as its nearest rival and many times cleaner than most plants.

Sunlaw was created by a man named Robert Danziger. As an industrialist, he is hard to classify. He's had previous lives as a jazz musician and scientist at the Jet Propulsion Laboratory. He is a large man, very large, and when standard golf clubs didn't fit him he designed his own. The living room of his house has been converted to a sound studio.

After World War II, this city was full of entrepreneurs like Danziger, men who habitually poked into the margins of things, making and sometimes losing several fortunes in their lives. Now, most of them are gone.

But Danziger remains.

. . . .

Ronald Reagan himself could not have dreamed up a better example of capitalism at work. No public monies had been spent. The air gets cleaner, toxics get reduced and jobs get created.

—Robert A. Jones, *Los Angeles Times*

- - - - - - - - - -

"Bob Danziger is a visionary. His willingness to take financial, personal and political risks to develop cleaner better energy technologies resulted in redefining 'best' in best available technology. Without Bob's commitment to our ecological future we would clearly have a less healthy environment."
—**Hon. Leon G. Billings**, *MD House of Delegates, Chief of Staff to Senate Majority Leader Ed Muskie and principal author of the Clean Air Act*

- - - - - - - - - -

"Bob was a one-man think tank for GE in the 1980s."
—**Lorraine Bolsinger,** *General Electric Vice President for Ecomagination*

- - - - - - - - - -

"Seeing you at the Air Resources Board the other day and hearing your perspective on your upcoming retirement, I felt compelled to drop you a few lines to acknowledge your contribution to cleaning up the air.

From the days of working with you while I was at the South Coast Air Quality Management District, it has been a great pleasure to see the tremendous progress that you had orchestrated through Sunlaw and the research and development being performed with the creation of Goal Line. You were always committed to reducing emissions from stationary sources to the maximum extent possible. The demonstration you have carried out at your powerplant has surprised many people and delighted many others, myself included. The continuing advances in this technology for stationary source applications and the extension to mobile source applications provides us with great encouragement for the future. The outstanding performance of the technology operating over a long time has made believers out of skeptics to the point at which it seems that the measurement techniques have not kept pace with the ability to control the emissions. What a wonderful accomplishment!

Bob, we are wishing you a long and active retirement. I also want you to know that you have made a major impact in advancing state-of-the-art emissions controls. Your personal commitment, perseverance, financial support and dedication to do the right thing will benefit many for years to come. Please accept my humble thanks and congratulations.

With very best wishes,"

—**Alan Lloyd**, *Chief Scientist, South Coast Air Quality Management District; Chairman, California Air Resources Board; and Secretary, California Environmental Protection Agency*

- - - - - - - - - -

"Bob Danziger is truly a person whose thinking is outside of the box. I became aware of biology. Subsequent conversations ranged from the problem of global warming and the generation of alternative forms of energy. Bob introduced me to microbial fuel cells, a process by which electricity can be generated by a variety of different microorganisms. It was clear that Bob, whose vast experience in energy production was intrigued by the phenomenon, and he suggested that we put together a small version of one commonly used type of fuel cell. We did using microorganism found in soil, mulch and manure. Now, here is one of Bob's thinking out of the box ideas, "Why don't we see if we can generate electricity from the non-carbon parts of coal?" I thought this to be a very odd idea, but when I read that certain species of bacteria live in coal I realized that he might be on to something. What I don't know whether he was aware of the coal-eating bacteria or was it his canny mind that led him to the idea. In brief, we were able to generate electricity from coal without combustion and went on to improve our fuel cell design to produce greater amounts power. I relate this story as only one example of the strength of Bob's thinking. One learns this within one's contact with this extraordinary person."

—**Paul Levine**, *retired professor, Stanford, Harvard, and Washington Universities*

- - - - - - - - - -

"I met Bob through a mutual friend, who thought Bob's and my shared interest in environmental science might lead to some interesting chemistry. Well it was like alchemy with our meeting leading to a collaboration, friendship and golden moments and golden accomplishments. Bob's knowledge and grasp of environmental issues led to me to ask him to give a guest lecture in my class in marine pollution. And his interest in the class, the students and the subject resulted in his semester-long participation and an incredible experience for the undergraduate, graduate and post-doctoral students taking the course. Indeed, this led to his being recruited as a co-instructor with me when the course was offered the next year.

What Bob brings to the table is intensity, commitment and creativity. Intensity and commitment were clear in his quick mastery of the regulatory issues on the government side, with Bob easily digesting an immense literature on the legislative, advisory and political side of marine pollution issues. This combined with his knowledge and experience on the business side of these issues provided a wealth of experience to the class.

Creativity is the other important side of interacting with Bob. I recount one example that has been extremely important in my research and teaching. It was Bob's reframing of my research area. This area is on a cellular mechanism for keeping pollutants out of cells. My fellow scientists refer to these as efflux transporters, as molecular motors that act to pump pollutants out of cells. Bob reframed the way the entire field now talks about this mechanism. What Bob called them was "bouncers." And this is now how all my colleagues refer to them. It is a brilliant metaphor, easy for the listener to understand that these are indeed bouncers, but instead of ruffians, the bouncers are keeping toxic things out of the cells. This renaming, reframing, recasting is an important aspect of Bob's creativity. It is his quickness in understanding complex issues and then creating a simpler way of looking, understanding and solving the problem at hand."

—Dave Epel, *Jane and Marshall Steel Professor of Biological and Marine Sciences, Stanford University*

- - - - - - - - - -

"Bob is truly the pioneer of our current private electricity infrastructure in the United States and Australia. He has pushed for open accounting in the power generation groups and pushed for environmental awareness and accountability back when the other companies pushed against it. Bob was instrumental in making Los Angeles's air cleaner and made it a much better place to live and work for hundreds of people. Many of those were children that needed that helping hand.

Bob can do anything he puts his mind to but more importantly, he has taken on many tasks that people say cannot be done, but he gets them done. It has always been a pleasure working for and with Bob on

many projects and task over the last 20 plus years. I would recommend Bob for any project but highly recommend him for the nearly impossible project!"
—**Tim Smith**, *Vice President, Wellhead Electric*

- - - - - - - - - -

"I first met Bob when a friend who was playing in his band around ten years ago invited me to a gig. From there I have used Bob as a percussionist on two albums in the last three years and was absolutely impressed with his ability to elevate any given theme to a level of greatness and the never ending supply of unexplored sonic landscapes."
—**Reinhold Mack**, *music producer*

- - - - - - - - - -

"Bob's sound sculpture, 'Nocture 1910,' has been the audience hit of 'Made in Monterey,' our 50th anniversary exhibition. Danziger's keen intellect, savvy technical expertise and wit produce an audio component which made our late 19th and early 20th century paintings come alive. This fruitful collaboration has proven to be a model for how we approach all future exhibition projects."
—**Michael Whittington,** *Director, Monterey Museum*

- - - - - - - - - -

"I've recently renewed a working relationship with Bob that began in 1978 when JPL was helping lead the early U.S. efforts to develop renewable energy and hybrid vehicles, hoping to solicit his help in defining meaningful roles for JPL in the alternative energy arena. His insights, broad background, and real world experience and perspective have proven even more valuable than I had hoped. And his grasp of both the big and the small—global and local—perspectives was amply evidenced at the labwide JPL seminar he gave here recently."

—Bob Easter, *Manager, Program Development Studies, JPL*

- - - - - - - - - -

"Bob Danziger brings tremendous value to the table, including a unique combination of creativity, deep knowledge and seasoned experience in the alternative energy and environmental technology industries. I greatly admire his dedication to developing clean energy solutions, as well as his integrity and generosity—all of which are borne out in his numerous successes and recognitions in business and in life. It is no mistake that this Renaissance man has been termed brilliant. Bob is an antidote to the business as usual that has helped bring us to this climate change juncture, and a model for the kind of businessperson we need in this age. I highly recommend this wise man and exceptional person."

After reading the book:

"I've finally been able to read your draft manuscript— I read most of it night before last and then nibbled at bits and pieces of it on my way to and from work on the metro until, sadly, it was all gone. Bob, this is incredibly funny. You're a great storyteller. This is going to be a great book and it will sell.

In addition to being incredibly laugh-out-loud funny, your stories inspire. They will inspire folks trying to make their way in the sustainable energy and environment world, but also anyone who's trying to follow their heart, be authentic and make a difference. What a gift.

Thank you for sharing it with me."
—**Montina Cole**, *Counsel, Schiff, Hardin LLP*

"Bob is many things—a true renaissance man. A former client of mine, I have found Bob to be great to work for, and work with. He is beyond bright, a great strategist and an outstanding musician. I can always rely on Bob to want to do the 'right' thing. He is truly selfless. In the years that I've known him, I've found Bob to be a truly inspirational human being. We've continued a friendship, and Bob is one of those very few people that cause me to say, 'I'm really glad to know that guy.'"

—**Mark Abramowitz**, *President, Community Environmental Services*

"It has been my privilege to know and work for Bob as a legal advisor for over 20 years. Throughout this time, Bob has impressed me as one of the most innovative, principled and thoughtful individuals I have ever encountered. As the CEO of Sunlaw Energy Corporation, he created and managed two cogeneration plants in Vernon, California, that were among the most efficient, safe and clean facilities that have ever been operated. In addition, as the co-founder of Goal Line Environmental Technologies (now known as

EmeraChem, LLC) he was the originator of some of the most environmentally effective technologies that have been created to reduce the harmful emissions from power plants. Bob to his credit has always put the environment ahead of his own business and financial interests and his tireless efforts to improve the air quality in Southern California through the use of innovative technologies have been well documented.

Rarely am I impressed by anyone but Bob is unique in marrying ethical business practices with concerns for the environment with an overall view to exponentially improving the health of our children and generations to come. I applaud him for all he is done and no doubt will accomplish in a career that has no horizons or boundaries."
—**Nicholson Thomas**, *Partner, Gibson, Dunn & Crutcher LLP*

- - - - - - - - - -

"My Dear Bob Danziger, your book is a hoot! When I read, I keep a notebook by my side but after making a dozen or so notes, decided to just read. And let me tell you, it made my day and a half. I'm a fast reader but found myself slowing down, so as not to miss anything.

There were lots of sweet moments. I loved your discussion on music and how it attracted deer and other animals. It should be a film.

You are a very, very funny man and adorable, to boot. Thanks for sharing, dear heart. And thanks for being such a wonderful friend and champion of Los Angeles history."
—**Carolyn Cole,** *Founder, Shades of LA*

Bob's an imaginative guy with a diverse set of talents including music, law, business, engineering and science. He blends several decades of experience in these areas into one package.
—**Brent Constantz,** *CEO Calera Corporation*

"Bob is one of the great business partners imaginable. He brings tremendous intellect, creativity, and energy to every project. His word is his bond, and loyalty and trustworthiness are among his strengths. We have been through good times and turbulent seas together and I look forward to the next opportunity to work together."

—**Bob Hilton**, *Vice President, Business Development, Alstom Environmental Control Systems*

- - - - - - - - -

"Bob is my top Smart Grid advisor, senior management consultant and reference energy expert, perfectly balancing these roles throughout his engagement with National Semiconductor. His superlative, out of the box strategic thinking, the experience of decades in executive roles in the energy industry, always dreaming of new possibilities and new worlds in the realms of both technology and business—are only matched by an exceptional insight into organizational, business and product development, and executive and board-level stellar influencing skills. Bob is a wonderful person to be around, he is the perfect mentor—his advice is invaluable to my business, and my personal and professional development."

—**Lucian Ion,** *National Semiconductor, General Electric*

- - - - - - - - -

If you've ever wondered when and why the original pronunciation of the planet Uranus ("Your Anus") was changed to the arguably more genteel sounding "Urine Us," this could be the book for you. If you're not in the mood for yet another scientific explanation of anything, better yet. But if you'd fancy being "a fly on the water cooler" . . . of the "Fly by Uranus" Voyager space mission that spawned the unceremonius name change as a public relations afterthought . . . this is definitely the book for you . . . scientists without the science and, as you will learn from the chapter in "Your Anus," sometimes without even pants.

Bob Danziger remembers the lighter moments that punctuate every human endeavor, in his case the serendipitous journey from musician – to college dropout (Bob left after three months to join an experimental band) – to experimental musician – to law school graduate – to space law pioneer – to energy cogeneration consultant – to clean air industrialist – to large wood sculptor – to scientific environmental thinker at large – and back. Instead of pursuing music as a full-time career, Bob brought his unique musical perspective to his many competing interests – space, energy, community financing of projects never done before, to name a few. To be sure, Bob provides an overview of the evolution of the private sector energy business that was born and has grown up in the last thirty years. His company, Sunlaw, is credited by many as the pioneering private sector energy company. Fiercely combining work with play, Bob none-the-less learned his lessons the hard way. Many in the energy establishment resisted Sunlaw's catalytic converter technology (adopted by the EPA under President Clinton as the industry standard), which put cleaner air out of the stacks than the atmosphere it entered, at a cost of pennies. Some among those with no interest in clean air called Bob "the most hated man in the energy business." Fortunately for the reader, Bob chooses to remember only the good times.

If you want to delve into the politics of the energy business there are other books that go there. For the meat and potatoes of energy science, you could read one of the papers Bob continues to present at institutional think tanks such as Stanford and the Jet Propulsion Lab at CalTech. But for those who wonder what a person like Bob was thinking at the start of their unique journey, I offer the inlaid inscription on Bob's giant Purple Heart Wood sculpture that graces the entrance of my home. Lifted from Bob's resignation letter to the band that swept him out of Antioch

College thirty plus years ago, as a kind of "sneak preview" of what was to follow, the inscription reads:

> "Where complexity melts
> to reveal alternate proposals
> irregular in shape
> but remaining as a window
> Through which you must leap."

Bill Straw—*Blix Street Records, March 2010*

- - - - - - - - -

"As Chairman Emeritus of the South Coast Air Quality Management District (SCAQMD), I was dismayed to hear that Sunlaw has been forced out of business; its equipment sold and sites razed. This is a major loss for all air breathers in southern California and the fight for clean air all over the world for a number of reasons:

Sunlaw was the most co-operative powerplant or industrial facility in the history of the SCAQMD, its facilities were always open and friendly to inspections, data requests and even going so far as to volunteer data, time and personnel.

Sunlaw was by far the most aggressive powerplant or industrial facility in the history of the SCAQMD in reducing emissions whether required to or not. I know that you have been the driving force behind this positive attitude not only in thought but in deed.

I have found Sunlaw, over its entire 16 years of operation, to be scrupulously honest and competent with respect to its emission monitoring equipment, personnel, procedures and use of the highest integrity independent testing companies.

I also know that the new emission control technology known as SCONOX would not be here today if it had not been developed by you and your team who were unwilling to use old ammonia based polluting technology because of your commitment to clean air.

The SCONOX technology, as first developed by Sunlaw, demonstrated 2.0 ppm NOX on a 3 hour rolling average basis and was declared to be Best Available Control Technology (BACT). It was declared so twice by the US EPA as being capable of achieving the lowest emission rate for all classes of gas fired turbines. Even more remarkable, these new emission standards were set without the use of ammonia. I am also aware that the SCONOX technology continues to demonstrate thousands of hours of commercial operation at 1.0 ppm or less NOX at numerous installations throughout the United States.

As I closely followed Sunlaw over the last 10 years, in addition to the subsequent maturity of the SCONOX product, I have concluded that SCONOX has never received credit for the absence of ammonia emissions and subsequent formation of particulates, from power generating facilities, nor the fact that the technology virtually eliminates many other hazardous air pollutants. The reason for such a lack of recognition is a mystery to me, considering the vast amount of data and requests given to the SCAQMD and the US EPA.

What saddens me most was the failure of the Nueva Azalea Project proposed by Sunlaw. This Project was, by a wide margin, the cleanest powerplant ever proposed in the history of the SCAQMD, and to the best of my knowledge, the cleanest of its type ever proposed in the world.

If it had been aggressively supported by both the SCAQMD and the California Energy Commission, a new standard for clean power generation would have been set, once again elevating the SCAQMD to the world leader in applying new technologies for cleaner air.

As Sunlaw closes down their operation, I would like to commend you for your personal and financial commitment (and mostly for your courage) in attempting to develop clean and efficient power generation in southern California and around the world. The SCAQMD is losing a great ally and friend.

I wish you all the best of luck in the future and consider my past relationship with you and your people to be one of the bright spots in my career.

Very truly yours,
Henry W. Wedaa
Chairman Emeritus
South Coast Air Quality Management District"
—**Henry Wedaa**, *Clean Air Pioneer*

Dedication

This book is dedicated to
Dr. Martha Drexler Lynn Danziger
my wife, friend, and love

How We Met

A party was thrown by Sara, a friend who produced
Fried Green Tomatoes. I didn't know I was going to a
party for her single friends—I thought I was going to a
business meeting.

Sara had invited a guy who worked at the same place
as Martha, hoping they would spark, and she invited a
fellow producer-person for me to meet. The producer,
though, showed up at the dinner with a boy-toy thirty
years her junior who was appearing in her new movie.
The dinner table had a glass top, but Miss Producer
and her friend apparently didn't care that the groping,
moaning, and other intimate communications between
them were happening in full view of the eight others at
the table. At one point, Martha looked at them after a
particularly moist exploration and said, "Please don't
pass the bread."

At the time I had two sprained ankles from a fall in Big Sur. After dinner, Martha sat next to me. The rest, as they say, is history. Martha would have me note it took almost three months to call, but it all has worked out beyond my wildest dreams, and I expect to be forgiven in my next lifetime if I come back as Martha's cat.

I knew I had to marry Martha when she volunteered to check my vacation cabin for mice, which I am really scared of. I'm the classic giant-who-jumps-on-the-table-if-there's-a-mouse kind of person.

When I asked Martha to marry me, I had an especially nice bottle of wine—even though I rarely drink—which I had saved, and I brought it over. It was a very old bottle and the cork fractured when I tried to open it, spraying me and my white shirt with a classic Bordeaux. I lived across the street from Martha and told her that I had to go home and change my shirt. She says that's when she knew something big was up, because I don't normally notice a dirty shirt.

I hurried back across the street with a clean shirt and a strong resolve. I was just about to ask her to join me on the back porch, pour some wine, and pop the question, when the doorbell rang. New neighbors had moved in the day before and decided that was a good time to introduce themselves. We chatted for about three minutes before I told them I didn't want to be rude, but there was something I needed to do right then, and we'd be over as soon as we could the following day.

They left, and as I was getting regrouped and reorganized the doorbell rang again. It was another new neighbor, asking if she could borrow a guitar cord! I said sure, ran across the street with her, gave her a handful of guitar cords, said a quick good-bye, and hurried back to Martha's.

She said yes.

Acknowledgments

The "LM Fraternity" is the group of people who more or less started the alternative energy/renewable energy/energy efficiency movement that is now growing into a trillion-dollar industry. This group is responsible for saving twelve billion barrels of oil and twenty-six billion tons of CO_2—and counting. It is still the largest energy and CO_2 conservation event in history. It is a reason for hope, and the millions of people pouring into the alternative energy industry can be helped by knowing about it.

The history of the who, how, and why of this extraordinary set of events has not been written. This posting is a small contribution to the record. I hope that others will add to this record to make it more complete, and to share points of view other than my own.

Starting in the early 1980s, by far the largest energy conservation program in history has been the switch from oil, and some coal, to natural gas for power generation, and the dramatic improvement in gas-fired power plant efficiency that started with the success of Sunlaw's independent power projects in Los Angeles.

Instead of the inefficient old industrial engines using bottom-of-the-barrel bunker oil first used by the nascent private power industry, Sunlaw went its own way in its search for ultra-high efficiency. It used the new engines that made jumbo jets possible and combined them with steam turbines to make the most electrically efficient utility power plants in the world. Revolutionary financing and risk management programs were invented. Technical and economic records were smashed. Copycat projects spread like a gold rush around the globe.

Sunlaw established the primacy of electrical efficiency and directly led the push for ever-greater electrical efficiency that has resulted in GE and Siemens products that are more than 55 percent efficient, and now approaching 60 percent in efficiency. Ultra-low emissions technologies have combined with these unprecedented efficiency gains to levels beyond our wildest dreams.

The "LM Fraternity" made this happen. "LM" stands for Land and Marine, the part of General Electric and Stewart & Stevenson that Sunlaw called upon to be the key supplier for this effort. There is much merit to the view that although they did not lead the effort, their long-term role has been the more crucial.

About the same time, Jim Heath and Jacek Makowski were establishing the wind and small hydro technology, business, and financing techniques that have now seen a firestorm of growth around the world. Many people crossed between Sunlaw and these other efforts, especially in financing and risk management.

I was the founder and CEO of Sunlaw and saw all of this firsthand.

There are many who deserve real credit. The group was far fewer than a thousand people total, and probably fewer than one hundred of them were the real visionaries and leaders. I've listed those I can remember below. These are some key people without whom this wouldn't have happened. The millions who now work in the industry and the billions who are praying for their success owe these people everything.

Ross Ain, Roger Feldman, Larry Kellerman, Joe Manning, Ron Spoehel, Al Smith, and Rick Stewart deserve special mention because they were ahead of me when I came to the scene and contributed the key concepts I used. Most were also vital to the growth of the industry after Sunlaw faded.

All my best wishes to you and your family for energy independence and a clean environment coupled with prosperity

The People Who Made It Happen

I know I'm missing some people, some of whom I should know and some I never knew about. I apologize profusely for any oversights.

Key early players (in alphabetical order by company and with the original affiliation):

- Bank of America: Ron Spoehel, Dick Mandabach

- AG Becker: Tom DePre, Bill Pope, Paul Rapisarda, Barry Friedberg

- Drexel Burnham: Don Kendall

- FERC: Ross Ain, Charlie Curtis, Adam Wenner

- GE: Brien and Lorraine Bolsinger, Dick Cull,

Bill Ferrell, Bob Rosencrance, Jack Welch

- Gibson, Dunn: Woody Woodland, Herb Krause, Nick Thomas

- Gillin, Scott: Joel Simon

- John Hancock/Energy Investor Fund: Margaret Stapleton, Barry Welch, Herb Magid, Jim Heath

- Hawker-Siddeley Power Engineering: John Cummings, Sonny Harkins, Lawrence Debbage, Herb Cook

- JPL: Richard Caputo, Jeff Smith, Donna Shirley, Richard Davis, Jerry Kasper

- Lloyd's of London: Peter Nottage, Richard Irmas

- Nixon Hargraves: Roger Feldman

- Power Systems Engineering: Al Smith

- Rocky Mountain Institute: Amory Lovins

- Shah, Vierra: Art Skilman

- South Coast Air Quality District: Henry Wedaa

- Stewart & Stevenson: Joe, Joe Jr., Carsey, and Jay Manning; Rick Stewart, Mark Axford, Gene Kelley, Don Wallin, Pete Watson, Steve Huval, Dan Stinger

- Sunlaw: Joe and Shirley Danziger, Woody Woodland, Destiny McHune, John Baum, Roger DeVito, Jay Lobit, Mark Sehnert, Mike Martin, Tim Smith, Gene and Carolyn Kelley,

- U.S. Senate, Chief of Staff to Majority Leader: Leon Billings

- Southern California Edison: Larry Kellerman, Ed Meyers, Mike Vogeler, Ron Luxa

- U.S. Growers Cold Storage: Sam Perricone, Angelo and Kathy Antoci

Some of these friends and colleagues have passed away, including May Joe Danziger, Herb Cook, Dick Cull, Dick Mandabach, Carsey Manning, Ed Meyers, Peter Nottage, Al Smith, and Dan Stinger, may they rest in peace.

One of the few histories of this area can be found at the *Project Finance Magazine* website: http://www.projectfinancemagazine.com/default.asp?Page=20&PUB=157&ISS=10992&SID=434401

In addition to these true pioneers, I acknowledge and thank the following people:

Jody Allione, Mark Abramowitz, Arno Baernhoft, Cheryl and Ron Barassi, Bob Bibb, Gary and Valerie Bird, Joe Blocker, Tee Bosustow, Douglas Brooks, Larry Campbell, Rich Caputo, Rob Carver, Catwoman, Shirley Danziger, Jack Douglas, Dave Epel, Curt Erickson, Senator Marta Escutia, Neil Feineman, Lois Gerard, Dave Gordon, Grant Harlan, Larry Harris, Cliff Hugo, Lucian Ion, Russell Ives, Buzz Joseph, Bob Jones, Charles Heckman, Bob Hilton, David Holman, Cliff Hugo, Tod Hunt, Ian Gardner, Juan Ibanez, Toby Kasavan, Mike Kazaleh, Theresa King, Norma Jean and David Keyston, Vinod Khosla, Alex Kinnier, Darcy Kopcho, Carolyn Kozo-Cole, Herb Krause, Albert Lee, Mike Levin, Paul Levine, Suzy London, Sinclair Lott, Roger Love, Julian and Reinhold Mack, Julian Mack, Fred Mandel, Mike Martin, Richard Mazur, Luis and Jules Mejia, Helcio

Milito, Harold and Paul Miller, Mike Miller, Rudy Ng, Cody Oliver, Jaci Pappas, Ronna Perelson, Senator Richard Polanco, Tom Preece, Jim Reece, Boris Reyes, Carol Rutan, Deborah Silgueros, Tim Smith, Greg Surman, Karl Sun, Bill and Lois Straw, John Thi, Eloy Torres, Joe Turnesa, Malcolm Weintraub, Mike Whittington, Bernie Wire, and the entire Woodland family.

5232790R0

Made in the USA
Lexington, KY
18 April 2010